To Daddy,

wishing you a
Happy Birthday
and lots of amusement.
Love Boris —

x   John

CONSTANTLY IN PURSUIT

Constantly

By the same author

AN IRISHMAN'S DIARY

A LONG DRINK OF COLD
WATER

A SHORT TROT WITH A
CULTURED MIND

LIFE IN THIN SLICES

PATRICK CAMPBELL'S OMNIBUS

COME HERE TILL I TELL YOU

HUTCHINSON OF LONDON

in Pursuit

PATRICK CAMPBELL

Drawings by

QUENTIN BLAKE

HUTCHINSON & CO. *(Publishers)* LTD
178-202 Great Portland Street, London, W.1

London Melbourne Sydney
Auckland Bombay Toronto
Johannesburg New York

First published 1962

*This book has been set in Bembo type face. It has
been printed in Great Britain by The Anchor Press,
Ltd., in Tiptree, Essex, on Antique Wove paper.*

Contents

Contents

ACKNOWLEDGEMENTS

The articles collected into this book first appeared in *The Sunday Times, The Spectator*, and *Go*. The author is grateful to the editors of these papers for giving permission for the articles to appear in book form.

I

Curzon Street on Thames

I T'S a romantic old riverside coaching inn, and its name and situation are as firmly welded together as smoked salmon and fillet steak.

It's called the Old Bell at Bulford. It can also be called the Old Bull at Belford, but whichever it is it's as much as your status is worth to drop one name without the other.

The very sound of the Old Bell at Bulford creates its own brand image. (If there is a place called Bulford which contains an Old Bell I'm talking about the Old Bull at Belford, and vice versa.)

The brand image is based upon 'driving out of Town for lunch' or 'popping in for a bite after the races'. It's a place to be travelled to in cars costing more than £2,000. (If it was the Old Bell *tout nu* it's the pub on the corner, which is approached on foot or by bicycle.)

The frontage of the Old Bell at Bulford is gleaming white plaster with shining black beams, and the only indication that it isn't a property dealer's private retreat from the rigours of Park Lane is a single sign of impeccably heraldic taste, designed and executed for 300 guineas by the art department of a distinguished advertising agency.

Chiffon, looped and draped in old English cottage style, veil the upper windows, where every bedroom contains hot and cold water and persons of wealth and breeding outwitting private detective agencies.

The entrance is at the side, affording a breathtaking glimpse of an old English garden, as lovesome and trim as anything at the Ideal Home Exhibition. But step inside, me Lord, and you're done.

9

Outside, the sun has not yet set upon the long spring evening. The last slanting rays lend a strange, exciting radiance to the tulips, the lawns and the river. But here, inside the Old Bull or Bell or Hell, we're damn' nearly in pitch darkness, as though it were the middle of the night in a flash shebeen in Curzon Street. Everything is, indeed, precisely similar to Curzon Street. Peach lighting behind the bar, carpets to the armpits, Grik *maître d'hôtel*, Italian beach-boys in white coats making like waiters until the American matron rough-shooting season breaks out in Portofino.

Six and sixpence for a doubtfully large gin and tonic while the Grik *maître d'hôtel*, hefting as best he can a two-foot-square menu, tries a soft-sell on the Sole Normande. 'I tail you, sir, I have something vairy special, just for you. . . .' At the other end of the bar the victor in a take-over battle pats the leg of an outwardly— and probably inwardly—bored piece of shorthand from the office. 'They do me very well here,' he tells her, having just fallen for the Sole Normande, ten days frozen and seventy miles from the sea.

Outside, the sun is going down in rare splendour behind the column of poplars, marching by the bend in the river. A white cabin-cruiser drifts by, looking for a 'No mooring' sign at which it can tie up for the night. The birds are singing their evening song.

But inside, me Lord, you're being shown to a table in an alabaster-white, brocade-curtained dining-room, each table with its own red-shaded, electric candle, and the river could be as far away as the sea. No bird sings, only the hushed rasping of heavy business men clinching deals, the strained chatter of family parties rendered nervous by the thought of Dad's bill for this foolish treat and, loudest of all, the silence of the couples, out-witting the detective agencies, from whom all sense of pleasurable adventure has been beaten by this thick, rich, concealed-lighting, urban, Curzon Street gloom.

That's what goes on, at prohibitive cost, inside the Old Bull at Belford, that romantic old coaching inn which looks so captivating from the outside. And that's why, with increasing despair on my beat up and down the Thames Valley, I continue to look for the riverside joint which will do the river the kindness of allowing that the river is there.

If the joint be beside the river we do not want a peach-lit bar buried among the stables at the back. We want a bar with one long window and a balcony overhanging the river. We want dramatic floodlighting on the weeping willows and the dark, mysterious water, so that, with benefit to our souls, we can look out instead of in. And the same thing goes for the dining-room, however architecturally impossible it might be. A riverside joint should seem to float, like a ship, with windows that disappear, because it isn't as cold as all that in England all the time.

Let no landlord trumpet that he has this very thing before assuring himself that his bar *and* his dining-room overlook the river, and all his dining-tables too—not just the four in the window reserved for the friends of the Grik *maître d'hôtel*.

If it were ever to come about I'd abandon all status-creating patronage of the Old Bell at Bulford and travel joyously, even by bicycle, to the Riverama Rooms.

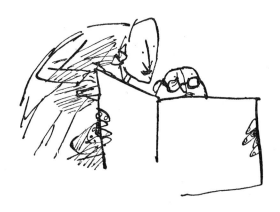

2

Underworld and Upper Crust

S ATURDAY night in a Chelsea pub and the whole caste on-stage—the suède jackets, the leather skirts, the knee-length jerseys, the black stockings—all mixed in and up with the stiff collars of the young lawyers, the mackintoshes of the Bradford poets, the raglan overcoats of the dog-walkers, the berets of the ancient painters, the Italian suitings of the advertising men—and all being served with fearful efficiency by three fresh-faced, teenage innocents arrived as recently as yesterday morning from Cork, Galway and Kinsale.

To retain one's position, and drink, at the bar was exhausting enough in itself, but we were faced with another hazard. A party was going on somewhere in the area to which we hadn't been asked but at which, two passing acquaintances informed me, the three of us would be more than welcome. The hazard lay in the act of buying enough refreshment for our own needs without allowing two suède jackets and a knee-length jersey to see what we were doing. Otherwise, it appeared, they would put two and two together and follow us to the house to which they hadn't been invited either, and trouble—unspecified, but certainly serious—would ensue.

One of the passing acquaintances, calling me 'Sir', suggested I do the buying while he and his friend distracted the attention of these undesirable elements—a fairly transparent device for avoiding payment of dues which Sir countered by buying half a bottle of spirits for himself and a quart of light ale for his new associates, only to be bouleversed a moment later by their return *in company with* the undesirable elements who, as it suddenly turned out, were the joint hosts and hostess of the proposed gathering and who furthermore had laid in so much to drink that there was no need for guests to bring their own.

I was still trying to get a rebate on my now surplus stock when the five new friends left, so I had to break off negotiations and run after them. Already the suspicion was forming that I might be too old—much too old—for this sort of thing, but after all it was Saturday night. . . .

The house was somewhere along the Embankment and the front door was wide open. No one bothered to shut it as we walked in and up the stairs to a flat with a large front room. It was in semi-darkness, with a record-player blaring. A number of young men—very young men—all, fairly obviously, upper crust, were leaning against the walls with expressionless faces, watching two couples doing the Twist. The twisters, oblivious to one another, performed their exertions with the remote concentration of boxers working out with skipping-ropes. There was very little talking. The young men outnumbered the girls by seven or eight to one. The atmosphere seemed to be one of brooding watchfulness, as though everyone were waiting for something to begin.

I went into the kitchen, in search of a glass. No one seemed to be drinking. The five earlier friends had disappeared. A feeling of middle-aged solitariness was setting in.

A girl, with an unsullied baby face and hair like a bleached busby, was sitting on the kitchen table, eating baked beans with a teaspoon out of a tin. She stopped when she saw me. 'Who are you?' she said, in the clear accents of Cadogan Square. 'You look like a dick.'

I straightened that out before the impression gained general acceptance. I offered her a drink. She looked at my half-bottle. 'Whiskey's a drag,' she said, and returned to her baked beans.

I went back into the sitting-room and leant against the wall for a while. Conditions were still notably short of anything approaching joy and pleasure. Everything too silent, too watchful, too pent-up for comfort. It could have been my nervous, middle-aged imagination but it seemed to me that all

13

these expressionless young upper crusters were waiting for something drastic, something violent, to begin—not knowing what it would be, but waiting just the same. . . .

When the five youths—sharp suits, oiled quiffs, winkle-picker shoes—burst in through the door it created an extraordinary yet almost invisible surge in the room. All the young men straightened up. They were taken by surprise, but they were glad, because something had started—at last.

A girl started screaming: 'Get out! You're not invited! Go away!' The leader of the new arrivals greeted her by her Christian name. One of the young men said, 'Be a good boy, Charlie—go away.' The upper crust and the underworld seemed to know one another very well.

Charlie looked round the room. The young men were closing in. 'You wouldn't want this nice little party broke up, would you?' I heard Charlie say, but that was the last thing I heard him say because in half the time it takes to tell I was down the stairs and out into the street and walking exceedingly briskly home, reflecting at the same time that the pleasures of the young seemed greatly changed since, dressed in white flannels and patent-leather pumps, I used to bring my ukulele to those tennis-club dances in the good, *good* old days.

3

Early to Bed, and Up Again at Once

Total rejection of and withdrawal from the harshness of the world—rockets, bombs, no post, Selwyn Lloyd's coming onslaught upon innocent business expenses, the overdraft and everything else—took place the other afternoon at 4.25 p.m. when this rejectionist went to bed. For the night, that is. In, permanently, until the following morning.

Conditions outside—wind, rain and more snow on Dartmoor. Conditions inside—approximate to those of a luxury nursing home, specializing perhaps in mental ailments in that I had to lock the door because the wind kept blowing it open. Oranges on the bedside table and a glass of milk, to guard against peckishness during the night. Everything snug and shut off. Curtains drawn, electric fire going, presentation hot-water bottles transforming the bed into a comfortable furnace. Everything ideal for a sixteen-hour withdrawal from the world and all its fearful works.

I finished my book—paper-backed copy of *Lolita*, not half bad—round about 5 p.m., already heavy-eyed, type blurring, sliding miraculously off into sleep—and this half an hour before the pubs were open for the evening session! I switched off the stove, the light, myself, letting the Sandman do his healing work. I woke with a snap thirteen hours later—six o'clock in the morning by my watch. Clear eyes, rested, ready for a really good day's work.

Sprang out of bed, eager to get on with it, and then noticed that the hot-water bottles were as hot as ever. The mind, refreshed, obtained an immediate grip on the situation. The usual, foolish error. It was, of course, not 6 a.m., but p.m. The Sandman had retained his grip but for a bare hour, leaving me with at least another twelve to go. And with nothing to read.

I was buying both evening papers on the corner of the street—slippers, trousers, mackintosh over pyjama jacket—when they caught me, roaring friends from Dublin over for the two-day meeting at Sandown Park. Swept helplessly into the pub, retaining my mackintosh with the greatest difficulty in the face of a blazing fire and back again into bed, sodden with stout, by 7.10 p.m. Mercifully, the second evening paper started to blur round about 7.45, and I went under for the second time, to awake, more clear-eyed and refreshed than ever, at 10.20, but realizing immediately, having been bitten once, that it was not morning but approximately the middle of the night.

I dickered for a while about getting up and going to the Establishment or some other night-spot, but decided it would undo the good that had already been done and the good that still remained to be done by health-giving sleep. After lying with eyes as blurred as searchlights, staring at the ceiling for an hour, I got up again and washed five pairs of socks. Then I cleaned the stove. Then I had a bath, reading while in it the medical section of *Pears Cyclopaedia*, gaining information I'd only guessed at before about diseases of the upper respiratory tract. I was back in bed, boning up on the care of ferrets—'probably a domesticated form of the polecat (*Mustela putorius*), known sometimes by that name and sometimes as *Mustela furo*'—by 12.30 a.m., after a heavy feed of bacon-and-eggs, to slip off into Slumberland for the third time that night about half an hour later.

I find it difficult to convey the sense of futility, of frustration, of bone weariness, of fundamental injustice I experienced when next my eyes snapped open and I found we'd only got as far as 3.55, having already had the equivalent of three nights' sleep in less than twelve hours. I got up and dialled TIM, in the feeble hope that my watch might have stopped, only to be told by that female insomniac at the other end that it was now three-fifty-six pree-cisely. 'What time will it be at the third stroke?' I asked her, short of someone to talk to. 'At the third stroke,' she said, 'it will be three-fifty-six and ten sec-conds.' 'Thanks a million. Good night.' I cleaned three pairs of shoes—the full spit-and-polish technique—and was back in bed again by 4.45, pretty well, after all I'd been through, tuckered out.

What woke me, fifteen minutes later—at five o'clock in the morning, that is—was the ringing of the phone. TIM calling me back! It couldn't be. But who—what . . . ? I'd a fearful struggle with the bedroom door, having forgotten I'd locked myself in. The phone went on ringing. At five o'clock in the morning. Beep-beep. Beep-beep. I staggered, bare-footed, into the sitting-room and picked up the receiver.

'Robin—that you?" A chatty, conversational voice. At 5 a.m.! 'Look,' it went on, showing a trace of concern, 'the doctor's rather kicking up about these tape-recordings . . .'

I couldn't take it in. It was beyond me. 'To whom,' I said somewhat stiffly, 'do you suppose you're talking?'

'That's not Robin?'

'No, it isn't.'

The voice took on a bitter, sarcastic note. 'Why don't you go back to bed, Dad? . . .' The receiver was slammed down at the other end.

He didn't know to whom he was talking—at all.

4

In a Common, Parisian Market

I T MUST have been the sound of the American voices that did it—slow, penetrating American voices overlaying the quick, penetrating French—that suddenly made me feel we were back in the roaring twenties, back in the days when Pappy Hemingway was around, and Scott Fitzgerald and Zelda, Gertrude, Ezra, Isadora, all the old gang—the sound of expatriate American voices in a bistro on the Left Bank in Paris.

It had to be allowed, however, that times had changed. The expatriates, as gay and as hard-drinking as their forbears, were now industrious foreign correspondents, political commentators, Common Market observers and directors of international advertising agencies, all accompanied by their legal wives and talking not so much about Dadaism, bull-fighting and the Actionalists as about President Kennedy, Katanga, Berlin and the oil set-up in the Middle East.

The aura was still there, though—the sound of American voices in a bistro on the Left Bank. So that when someone suggested we should move on and take in a few night-spots I was all for it. The feeling was very strong that the twenties were about to roar again.

The gang eventually narrowed itself down to four, including myself. The others had to be in the office early next morning, and in any case had long drives before them out to their houses in the country. (Wasn't Pappy shacked up in an attic in the Rue du Chat Qui Peche?)

We found a taxi, driven not by the traditionally vinous, garlic-reeking old veteran of the Marne, broken peaked cap, Gaulois singeing his walrus moustache, but by a brisk, clean-

shaven, bare-headed young man in a leather jacket who said he
rather doubted if many of the really amusing places would be
open during Christmas week but we could certainly try our luck.

The first two were closed. Notices on the doors promised
a grand gala on New Year's Eve but not tonight. The third one
was open. The entrance was ringed in blue neon lighting, suggesting pleasures of a similar nature inside.

We went in—one of the party, at least, prepared to be shocked
to the core of his Protestant being by a sudden blaze of *les nues*—
to find ourselves in a skilful representation of a Mayfair cocktail
bar. The room was crowded with dignified-looking French
business men sitting at tables with their dignified wives. Waiters
in white coats moved among them, serving drinks on trays. At
the far end of the room an impeccably dinner-jacketed pianist—he
looked like Hutch's grandson—was playing and singing a duet
with a girl in evening dress. Their voices were politely hushed,
but I caught the words—'It's June in January, because I'm in
love . . .' Their accents were pure Balliol and Girton, as indeed
was the accent of the barman. 'Good evening, ladies and gentle
men—and what is your pleasure?'

The expatriates ordered Scotch. To remove the debilitating
feeling that we were back in Curzon Street I asked for a pastis.
'And could you cash me a traveller's cheque for ten pounds?'

'Certainly, sir.'

I signed it, handed it over, and found a Savile-Row-suited
Frenchman at my elbow, Legion d'Honneur in the lapel. 'It is
easy to see,' he said, accent barely perceptible, 'that you are
English. In Paris it is only the English who drink pastis. For the
chic Parisian now it is always Scotch.' He sipped delicately at his
own. 'It is only south of Valence, on the Côte d'Azur, that pastis
becomes chic. You will forgive me telling you this? . . .' He drifted
away, as chic as chic, before I could tell him I was Irish, and give
him a few tips about the protocol of plain porter consumption
in Ballyhadareen.

I turned back to the barman and asked for my change from

the £10 traveller's cheque. He shrugged—actually shrugged—and moved away to the other end of the bar.

Cold, immediate rage set in. The rapacious French, at it again, and as obviously as ever. The merchant in the Savile Row suit, hired by the management to divert me with all this chat about Scotch, trying to make me forget I'd just handed over a cheque for £10.

I applied to the expatriates for help. I knew that a personal assault on the barman would cause him, as usual, to lose his grip on the English language and to reply in some Basque dialect so accusatory that I'd have to give him another £10 to keep him quiet.

The expatriates were helpful. They explained that my £10 just about stacked up to the cover charge for four persons, but that I was not to worry. They themselves had paid for the drinks.

A tenner, just to get into the Parisian conception of a Mayfair cocktail bar, with Balliol and Girton singing 'June in January' and a lot of French business men drinking Scotch!

The roar of the gay, rumbustious twenties died away to a whisper. A new age had arrived—the age of the Common Market. No more expatriates. We were all one.

I can only hope the new arrivals are going to be able to afford it.

5

Out in the Front Line

WRITERS, writing, should be hermetically sealed into the cocoon of their own imagination.

Writers, writing, should see only the characters of their own creation.

In this state of literary grace writers should be able to write anywhere, in attics, garrets, penthouses, doss houses, hen houses, gazebos, bordellos, in total intellectual isolation from their surroundings. There is, however, one place in which no writer can get on with anything and that is at a desk in a ground-floor window facing outwards when he happens to know a number of the people that live on the other side of the street. The characters of his own creation tend to pale into insignific——

Hello, hello, hello! And what have we been up to last night in No. 49? A little bit of a rout, by the look of it. Husband leaving for work only now, and it's already past ten. He's not in good shape at all. Moving very tentatively, as though he was walking on hot-water bottles. It's a grey morning, but the light seems to be hurting his eyes. They were at it, all right. Bedroom curtains still drawn, wife still comatose. Interesting——

It's a wrench to get back to my typewriter, to seal myself into the cocoon of my own imagination, to create dialogue for characters called Bert and Fred—particularly in view of the fact that the dry-cleaner's van has just stopped outside No. 53, the house with the two pretty daughters. If ball-gowns are going in they're going to a ball, if they're coming out they've been. They've been! Well, well. That's the worst of these long winter evenings, dark by four o'clock. One can't keep a check on things at all. . . .

Bert: Turn it up, Fred.
Fred: I never done it, Bert, so help me. . . .

They've let the dog out again in No. 51! It's that Portuguese—or Spanish—maid. She's a demon for polishing the door knocker, and the dog knows it. He lets her settle to her work with the door half open and then he's out like a flash and off down the road. Mistress will be after him any minute now, head-scarf round the hair-curlers. There she goes!

Bert: We don't want no punch-up, Fred, do we?
Fred: I tell you, Bert, Agnelli done it. . . .

Bedroom curtains pulled in No. 49! We've surfaced! Oh, dear, oh dear. Very, very pallid indeed. Our eyes meet across the street. She looks at me for a long moment, but sightlessly, without recognition. I'm about to wave, to give her some small message of cheer, an indication that things may be slightly better after lunch, but before I can do so she turns away, disappears.

This is a thing that baffles me. They all, all the people across the street, know I'm here. They see me framed in the window every day from ten till six; on duty, as it were. They know they cannot go in or come out or appear at any front window without my seeing them. Yet they never give the slightest sign that they're conscious of my presence. Or, at least, they didn't until the other day. Now things are very different.

It came about as a result of a party given by No. 51. During the course of it I fell into conversation with the dog-chasing girl. I'd met her only casually once or twice before, but now she seemed bent upon creating a closer relationship. 'Do forgive me,' she said, 'but I must speak to you. You see, I feel such a frightful nuisance all the time.'

It sounded like an interesting nobody-loves-me syndrome, heightened by vodka on the rocks. 'You mean,' I encouraged her, 'a frightful nuisance to the whole human race. You feel outcast, unwanted——'

'Good lord, no.' She laughed piercingly. 'I meant—to you. I mean, I'm rushing in and out all day and I can see you're concentrating frightfully hard on your work so I never know whether I should wave or not. I mean, sometimes I can't quite tell if you are working or not and if you're not I don't know if I shouldn't—well, you know—wave . . .'

'I tell you what you do,' I said. 'Every time we catch each other's eye you wave like mad. That way we won't make any mistakes.'

Next day we didn't make any mistakes at all. She must have been in and out about forty times, dog chasing, shopping, shovelling stuff into the dustbin, and we nearly waved our flippers off every time. And now the word's got round. On occasion it seems to me that every window across the street is filled with waving hands and beaming smiles. They're all suffering from a powerful sense of relief. Even the publican up the street has become infected. On his morning trek for lunch-time bread he waves like anything as he goes by.

The only way, it seems to me, that a ground-floor writer can wrap himself in the cocoon of his own imagination is by pulling the blind, or turning round the other way.

6

Over and Under the Yardarm

'WELL,' they say, 'you must have taken your holiday early. Where did you get that wonderful suntan? Capri, Majorca, Tenerife?'

The reply surprises them. 'That's London local, obtained from basking in backyards, areas, miniature roof gardens, balconies, attic windows and the sunny side of the street.'

They cannot believe it, their minds limited by the conventional concept of deck-chairs and the beach. It is pleasant to see their irritation. 'Backyards? Areas? You're as brown as that? Mine isn't nearly as good and I'm just back from two weeks in Villefranche. . . .'

They do not know of the dedication of the true urban basker, the dedication that drives us to follow the sun through the city from dawn to merciful dusk.

It's an extraordinary kind of mania, this hunger for the sun, as obsessional, as nerve-fraying as the addict's desire for gambling, drink or drugs. I haven't talked to a doctor about it, but it must be due to some psychological or physical deficiency like compulsive hand-washing or pregnant women chewing chalk. I only know that when the heat-wave strikes the city and the sun blazes down at eighty-two degrees I have to pursue it, dodging the terrible shadows of the buildings as though they were poisonous, all the time trying to keep the sun in sight until contact can be made with it only from some high attic window, as it sinks beyond the end of the Great West Road and the beginning of night brings peace.

It's a mania that makes, I can tell you, for a wearingly peripatetic kind of day, particularly if work also has to be fitted into the schedule.

The first two hours of the day are fine, altogether free of anxiety. At 7.30 a.m., already excitingly hot, the sun arrives in the backyard, allowing breakfast to be taken in conditions of uninterrupted roasting, apart from the gradual moving of the table and chair some eighteen feet to the left in order to keep Old Ra, as I've come to call him, blazing fair and square on the chest. But by 9.30 he's creeping away round the corner of the house, and the terrible shadow is advancing, as panic-provoking to the urban basker as water rising in a cellar in which he's trapped.

On with the clothes, cursing the necessity for them, over the bathing-trunks and a quick walk of about a mile, on the sunny side all the way, to the house of a friend in whose backyard Ra operates at full blast until 12.45 p.m. Out with the typewriter and off with the clothes, disregarding the outraged faces of people peering from windows, until Ra once again does his maddening vanishing trick behind the roof. Swift re-clothing and hurrying half a mile for lunch to a pub with a garden having a southerly aspect, from which Ra unhappily withdraws himself behind the chestnut trees twenty minutes in advance of closing time. But then there's another friend, the back of whose house faces west, so that camp can be set up in his sitting-room window. Out with the typewriter, off with the clothes, and then the anxiety of leaning farther and farther out of the window as Ra goes farther and farther round towards Shepherd's Bush until inch by agonizing inch he's gone again.

But then there's another pub, the front of which faces west, which has three small tables on the pavement, and the one on the end catches twenty-five minutes of the evening sun. I'm there, before opening time, to claim it. And round the corner, then, there's a little open square and on the bench beside the gate . . .

Mania indeed—a mania that causes the urban basker to face the wrong way in bus queues so that a little more patina can be added to the forehead—a mania that moves him to kneel on the floor of taxis, keeping a watchful eye on the driver, so that Ra can strike in through the open window and, unimpeded, do his work. The sun is a magnet, a hypnotist, a will-o'-the-wisp, the Pied Piper, the irresistible force that drags us urban baskers after him into areas, up to balconies, over roofs and even on to chairs, where we stand on tip-toe in backyards, keeping our heads, until the last second, above that terrible, creeping shadow which, when it strikes, amounts to the same thing as having one's supply of heroin cut off.

All this pressure, this constant bustle and rush, has one curious effect which will be, no doubt, a comfort to persons whose tan has cost them several hundred pounds on the Côte d'Azur.

The urban basker may be brown as a berry in front but he's always as pale as celery behind.

The conditions under which we live never seem to give us the time to baste both sides.

7

No Coins in the Fountain

TOTAL assets at 7 p.m. on a wet and windy night of fourpence in the pocket, two (breakfast) eggs and half a loaf in the larder, and a hunger valued at £1 10s.

The very edge of starvation, to be clawed back from only by the cashing of a cheque, but where was this to be done when the nearest cheque-cashing restaurant was an eightpenny fare away by bus?

There was, admittedly, an Indian establishment within running distance through the rain, but, to judge by its exterior, its circumstances were even more depressed than my own. I had already observed its tariffs, set forth on a menu glued with steam to the window: 'Mutton Curry, 2s. 3d., Lamb Curry, 2s. 6d., Prawn Curry, 2s. 9d.'

At these give-away prices an enormous order would have to be put in—mutton, lamb and prawn curry all together, with every available accessory—before the bill would be large enough to justify the presentation of a cheque. And say they refused to accept it, their suspicions reasonably aroused by this millionaire curry-fancier, short of 15s. 6d. in cash? Searched in the kitchen at the back and total assets of fourpence revealed? Certainly not.

The lack of money, I noted, accompanied by ravening hunger, promoted pessimism, the expectation of persecution, in a temperament normally free of such shadows. This, I saw, was the time to grasp the nettle, to make a bold move before an excess of humility wholly unmanned the spirit and left the body to starve. The thing to do—and quickly, before the supermarket closed at eight o'clock—was to bluff it out in the sombre-looking pub on the corner, one which I'd always passed by until now.

27

The raid began well. The saloon bar was empty, save for a young man behind the counter wearing a smart, dark suit. The manager, the landlord, lumbered by the brewers with this sad caravanserai for the purpose of testing his courage? Eagerly he folded his newspaper, glad to be back in business. 'Good evening, sir. Nasty night.'

'Good evening, landlord. It's even nastier than you think. I live just up the road—unaccountably short of currency—wallet dropped——' Halfway through it I saw he was ready to oblige. 'So if you could possibly cash me a cheque for five——'

'With pleasure, sir.'

'Wonderful.' Out with the cheque-book, rich, effective, persecution mania evaporated, hunger about to be satisfied, back on top of the world. 'Let's have a large Scotch as I'm here. And what about yourself?'

'Thank you, sir. I'll have the same.' Something of a blow, reducing my take by 8s. 8d., but even at that it was worth it.

He put my cheque in his pocket and rang open the till. After a moment he said: 'Well, that's awkward. The wife's lifted the float.' He held up a ten-shilling note. 'That's all there is.'

'Oh. You—you don't have any yourself?'

'Not a penny.'

'Neither do I.'

We were unable to conceal our mutual anxiety. By his estimate I owed him 8s. 8d.; by mine he owed me £4 11s. 4d. 'What are we going to do?'

'If you could wait a little, sir. The regulars'll be in soon. They'll make it up in no time. . . .'

Half an hour later we'd advanced towards our goal by 17s. 5d., mainly in halves of bitter, plus another 8s. 8d. on the slate from me for the same again for both of us. It seemed the least I could do.

Trading continued slow. A pint of mild and two stouts in the next half-hour. We agreed it was the fault of the weather. 'Night like this,' the landlord said, 'they'd rather be at home with the telly.'

I became, for the first time, keenly appreciative of the difficulties of the licensed trade, and even more so a moment later when a young man shot in with an empty siphon, claimed 7s. 6d. deposit and shot out again. The landlord failed to meet my eye. 'It used to be only six bob,' he said, 'but it's gone up.' To re-establish our confidence we had the same again.

It was the two jolly salesmen who saved us. Large gins all round and never mind the morrow. One of them paid for the last round with a five-pound note, and received his change. They left us to our vigil, but now the situation had cleared. It was with pride in the popularity of his public house that the landlord slapped down the fiver on the counter. 'There we are, sir,' he said. 'I thought it wouldn't be long.'

'Good man. What do I owe you?'

'Let me see. Six doubles. That'll be twenty-six bob.'

He took back the fiver and rang open the till. I could tell by his face what had happened. No change. We were, in fact, back to the ten-shilling note with which this long and interesting evening had begun.

8

Up Quasimodo, Down with Death

THE Metropolitan Music Hall in Edgware Road presented an all-in wrestling contest the other night between Quasimodo, the Hunchback of Nôtre Dame, and Dr. Death of Hollywood, U.S.A., billing it as 'the match that you thought you would not see', a pessimistic prognostication denied by a full house.

I was drawn, with a bag of roasted peanuts, to the scene of possible destruction myself, having been a passionate fancier of all-in work since the great pre-war days of the Ring at Blackfriars, where the last battle on the bill was often fought between two ladies in bathing-suits wrestling in mud—the mud being spread round the arena from a black coffin, labelled in white letters, 'By courtesy of Norwood Cemetery'. It made a pleasant change from the ceaseless round of art galleries, poetry readings and Promenade concerts.

As Quasimodo and Dr. Death stepped into the ring at the Metropolitan I saw that the fine old classical, knock-about tradition was being maintained.

Quasimodo—or 'Quassy', as he appeared to be known to his followers—was an elderly, dwarf-like citizen probably in his middle fifties, with four front teeth missing in the upper row. On his entirely bald head he wore a scarlet jester's cap, with bells, and a short, harlequin-patterned jacket in red and green with more bells dangling from its extremities. Red elastic knee-caps and red boots completed an ensemble owing not a great deal to Victor Hugo.

Dr. Death, when he arrived, did not seem to think much of it either. The Doctor, a figure of some menace in a large purple dressing-gown, with a skin-tight purple mask enveloping his whole head, walked over to Quassy's corner, examined him gravely and then turned to the audience, arms flung out in a gesture of incomprehension. The mask veiled the Doctor's features, but he was clearly asking us, 'What is it?' He turned back to Quassy and inspected him again, bending down to get a closer view. Quassy responded by gibbering at him and clawing the air. The audience, wearying of this not fearfully stimulating by-play, invited both of them to get on with it.

The Doctor stalked back to his corner and removed his dressing-gown, while retaining the mask. He revealed a figure having much in common with that of a large, stately butler.

Quassy disentangled himself from his jester's cap and tinkling jacket and did some more gibbering and clawing by way, apparently, of loosening up for the coming fight to the death. 'This bout,' the programme said, 'promises to be one of the fiercest contests ever seen here, as both these men have brought aggressive destruction down to a fine art.'

The bell went for the start of the first round. Dr. Death marched out from his corner, carrying his stomach high and well forward, very much the butler arriving with the information that dinner is served.

Quassy, gibbering and clawing, crouched in front of the Doctor, his stone-bald head about on a level with the Doctor's waist. Quassy now added a hissing sound to his limited repertoire of threats. At that moment a mournful voice rang out from the stalls, directed at Quasimodo, the Hunchback of Nôtre Dame. 'Come on, Passion,' it intoned wearily, 'do 'im.'

A great roar of laughter went up. It released us all. As the two elderly gentlemen in the ring tangled slowly and painfully with each other everyone in the theatre started shouting, all trying to match, to outdo, that splendidly mournful voice, all trying to gain the laughter of the whole theatre for themselves.

It was pretty poor stuff. No one could get near. 'Come on, Passion—do 'im.'

'Ring 'is bell fer 'im, Doctor.' A piping voice from a be-spectacled youth who'd presumably read Victor Hugo's master-piece.

'Keep Death off the road.' That didn't work either.

I started thinking furiously. The opportunity was too golden. The laughter of a whole theatre for the sake of a few words. . . .

Quasimodo. Nôtre Dame. I couldn't remember a word of it. Who was that girl? Esmeralda! He carried her up into the belfry, or something. Gargoyles. All too literary. I transferred my attention to Death. Walt Whitman. 'Come, lovely and soothing death, undulate round the world . . .'

'Undulate rahnd ole Quassy, Death!' Nothing like it. Nothing like it at all. What more about Death? Death of a Salesman. Death in the Afternoon. O Death, where is thy . . . ?

Dry-mouthed, all taut inside, lungs filled to bursting, I waited for the moment to let it go, for the moment when Quassy was on top with the Doctor upended. Then, the clear, derisive voice—'O Death, where is thy sting?'—followed by a great gale of laughter, applause. . . .

It occurred to me that 'thy' might sound a little affected in this milieu. 'O Death, where is *your* sting?' 'Hey, Death—where's yah sting?' I was still working on it when Quassy and the Doctor both fell down at the same time, marking the end of the contest.

But Death will fight again. Next time, perhaps, when I've got it right? . . .

9

Cosy, with Old Rubbery-Slubbery

THERE was no doubt about it the dogs, the trotters, the plates, the pedal extremities—anything is better than the fearful word 'feet'—were stone-frozen, and this after no less than a whole hour in bed, a time sufficient in normal circumstances for them to have generated a glow like a double-filament electric fire. A good strong boy, you see, accustomed to the rigours of the outdoor life, priding himself upon no overcoat in winter, upon a circulation roaring round like a mill-race.

I took a grip upon the bedrail, for additional purchase, and performed a series of *fouettés* in the prone position, twinkling the trotters round and about each other, aiming for an abrasive effect creating warmth. After a moment of this the breath became so short and the pounding of the heart so laboured that a halt had to be called before unconsciousness set in. The extremities remained stone-frozen. The mill-race circulation, now seemingly down to a trickle, seemed to die out somewhere above the knee.

It was old age, that's what it was—old age striking suddenly in the cold, silent night. Blue nose next, rheumy, weeping eyes, long underpants, grey woollen mittens, knitted pullover enclosed by a waistcoat, watch-chain dangling across the front, lumpy bedroom slippers, steel-rimmed spectacles, the knobbled, arthritic hand. . . .

Without warning, I began thinking about hot-water bottles. With eagerness, in place of the nausea that these floppy, sloppy, revoltingly old-maidenly cosy, rubbery-slubbery, feet-impregnated water-bags had always previously engendered. A hot-water bottle now would put the Grim Reaper back a year or two, take his scythe away from my feet. But good strong boys, accustomed to the rigours of outdoor life, don't own hot-water bottles, cannot tolerate hot-water bottles except in cases of serious illness, would not dream of having a hot-water bottle in the house.

On a sudden inspiration I got up and boiled a kettle and poured it into an empty wine-bottle and the wine-bottle cracked and starred all over, while retaining its shape. Boiling water spurted out, as though from a garden syringe. Then the bottle disintegrated and I spent ten minutes picking broken glass out of the sink, with the feet adhering to the icy linoleum of the kitchen floor. Subsequently a long series of *fouettés* in woollen socks created sufficient heat, combined with physical exhaustion, to permit of a restless sleep.

Next morning I was prowling up and down outside the windows of the largest chemist's shop I could find, peering in from time to time to see what was doing in the hot-water-bottle line. Large shop required for camouflage. No desire to make my request in a small one, where it might be overheard by elderly women buying elastic stockings, bunion pads, arch supporters or other buttresses against senility.

Just inside the door, I noted, in a large wire basket, were dozens of cheap hot-water bottles in red and blue, lying flatly one upon another and slithering about, when agitated, like dead plaice. They were small, hard, uncovered and—somehow—dull.

Now that I'd decided to buy a hot-water bottle, to take this dramatic, traumatic step from vibrant youth into chilly old age, I wanted a real, bang-up whizzer of a hot-water bottle, a big rough, tough hot-water bottle covered in genuine leopard-skin or made of tooled leather—a real man's hot-water bottle, a White Hunter's hot-water bottle that could be used on safari as a wine-skin, or even a svelte and elegant Noël Coward hot-water bottle, wrapped in a silken, Paisley dressing-gown or in the colours of the Brigade of Guards. . . .

'Didja want something?' The usual multiple-range-chemist's assistant, eighteen years of age, lavender-nylon working coat, the hair tipped, dipped, bleached and lacquered with the entire multiple-range from the cosmetic counter at wholesale prices. Extensive examination of pearly aluminium nails, and total lack of concern with the customer's requirements.

'Do you have any bittle botters than those?'

'I beg yah pardon?'

Nervousness had tangled my speech. I worked down through 'botter bittles' into 'better hot-batter battles' and eventually got home to 'better hot-bottles than those'.

'I could do you,' she said, 'a comfie or a quiltie,' putting us right into the middle of the old-maidenly, cosy-wosy, satiny-watiny area I'd been hoping to avoid.

I examined the comfies and the quilties, items in old rose and baby-blue. They were covered with a short, synthetic fur that felt like the skin of a shaved bull-terrier. I chose an old rose, she put it in a bag and I left, giving a youth buying a razor a hard stare. When I got the old rose home I found she'd forgotten to provide me with a stopper. I didn't feel like going back.

The nights are easier now. The wine-bottle cork stuffed into the neck of old rubbery-slubbery gives her—I mean him—a sort of masculine look, a quick, backwoodsmanlike improvisation against a sudden nip in the weather.

It makes it look as though I didn't really mean it after all.

10

If It Wasn't for the Others

CIGARETTES prohibitively expensive.
Pipe tobacco ludicrously cheap.
Result—easier breathing, cleaner palate, brighter eye, improved digestion, vertigo, bronchitis and lung cancer diminished.

What a wise recommendation upon the part of the Royal College of Physicians, one regarded by pipe-smokers everywhere as little short of genius. Not, of course, that there is the least hope of the recommendation being adopted. A fall in revenue is never regarded by any government as being counter-balanced by a rise in national health. Furthermore, legislation which gives one section of the community the tiniest crumb of advantage over another is regarded in these egalitarian times as a criminal assault upon the Rights of Man, despite the fact that, faced with a new law, the first concern of Man in the twentieth century is to evade it and secondly to turn it to his own profit. If neither of these objectives can be achieved he turns savagely upon those who are deriving, from the new law, their just and legal benefits.

Lobbying, of course, has already broken out against the pipe-smoker, taking that amorphous crew by surprise. It's probably fair to say that they never considered themselves to be a separate entity until a national newspaper—admittedly on a slack Saturday morning—devoted the whole of its leading article to establishing *apartheid* between pipe-smokers and the rest of human kind, familiarly denying at the same time the validity of its own conclusions. 'We repeat that there is, doubtless, no truth in the picture . . .'

The picture presented is bias run wild. 'The cigarette-smoker enjoys gaiety, talk, mixing openly with the herd. Pipe-smokers sit glumly apart, sucking their stems, ruminating on . . . what? How to engineer someone's downfall?' And much more. 'He clothes himself with the aroma of spurious authority which the slow, sententious stem-jabbing and all the other pipe-smoking paraphernalia lend him . . .' And so on and so on.

Pipe-smokers who read the piece recognized it immediately to be the work of a cigarette-sucker, all of whom are light-minded men given to jumping to facile conclusions.

The truth about pipe-smoking—and once a pipe-smoker lays down a truth it will be hours before he takes it back—the truth about pipe-smoking is that every pipe-smoker regards all other pipe-smokers as the root cause of the general unpopularity of pipe-smoking.

The crimes that all other pipe-smokers commit against the aesthetics of pipe-smoking seem to the true pipe-smoking crafts-man literally to be without number and so wide in variety that the only punishment he can inflict is that of smoking his own pipe unobtrusively—the very essence of the matter—back. By its nature the punishment tends to go unnoticed, thereby creating schisms and bitterness among what the cigarette-suckers regard as a stolid band of united brothers, puffing away in a haze of mutual admiration, whereas in fact it's all that one pipe-smoker can do to stay in the same room with another.

It's the other pipe-smoker who gives pipe-smoking a bad name. His equipment is an offence to every canon of good taste. The caddishness, the *palais-de-danserie* of pouches striped in regimental and old-school colours. The ostentation of pigskin, the medical-clinical look of transparent yellow plastic, when one knows that only a slim, clean, bakelite, screw-together container will do. It obviates, during filling, that miserly scuffling about, pipe buried in the pouch, that always puts one in mind of a man who carries his change in a purse and picks it over in the lid, hiding it from prying eyes.

All other pipe-smokers smoke pipes which are absurdly large or ludicrously small. They smoke pipes with bamboo stems or built-in plumbing, with meerschaum linings and even leather-covered bowls. They take them out of their mouths and look at them, holding them sideways between finger and thumb. They pass the bowls beneath their nostrils, apparently judging the aroma which they should be getting from the other end. They bring up the shine by rubbing them against their noses. Some of them keep their pipes in little velvet bags. Others store them in pipe-racks with 'My Lady Nicotine' burnt in poker-work along the top. They have a pipe for every day of the week and show them to people, very slowly, one by one.

All other pipe-smokers smoke a brand of tobacco which poisons one's own pipe for a week, if one should be sufficiently parsimonious to borrow a fill. It's also probably true to say that all other pipe-smokers clothe themselves in an aura of authority by slowly and sententiously jabbing with the stems of their pipes while the craftsman holds his quietly just astern of the canines, talking gaily round it, mixing openly with the cigarette-smoking herd from which—the thought goes off suddenly like a rocket—pipe-smoking is going to gain some interesting recruits, if the doctors have their way.

Women.

One has the feeling that one hasn't really seen anything yet.

A Table Wine for Removing Grease

L AST year's grape harvest must be in or the vintage come to fruition or something similar must have happened in the baffling world of wine because the town is alive these days with wine-tastings, ceremonies sufficiently corrosive to the teeth and stomach to put one off wine-drinking for ever, although a lot would depend, of course, upon how they are handled.

There was a particularly interesting one the other evening whereat a group of us wine aficionados were invited to adjudicate upon twelve bottles of Beaujolais, four of which were stated by the management to be of the approximate composition of nitric acid, a fearful threat to our well-being in view of the fact that the labels had been removed from the bottles so that they went only by numbers, thereby presenting no clue to the quality of the sauce inside.

Not, I have to allow, that the retention of the labels would have made very much difference to me. A Beaujolais, I always say, is a Beaujolais, a nourishing gulp that ought to retail round about 8s. 6d. It means nothing to me that some are shipped by and others are bottled by and still more are specially selected by. I don't mind if it's a Beaujolais Villages or Superior or Fleurie. They all taste fine while you're lashing them down and exchanging views with persons of contrary opinion about the ultimate fate of the human race.

This matter of the twelve numbered bottles had, however, no immediate connection with pleasure—rather, in fact, the reverse.

The management, in a sombre opening address, warned us that they had bought the four nitric acids at random from various off-licences and pubs around the town and that they, in fact, bore no relation to Beaujolais at all. The enormous increase in wine-drinking in this country had been leading the bottlers and shippers and others into sin. They were selling stuff under the name of Beaujolais suitable in the main for removing grease from the doors of ovens, and it was up to us to track down these detergents. We were issued with a score-card, a wine-tasting glass and the offer of palate-cleansing cheese-and-biscuits, and requested to get on with it.

We gathered round the first bottle, decorously helping one another to half an inch, holding out our wine-tasting glasses by the stems. We swirled it round and sniffed it and held it up to the light and sipped it and rolled it round our tongues. Some of the older and more expert players then spat their miniature mouthfuls into large boxes filled with sawdust, made a note on their score-cards and moved on to bottle No. 2.

For myself, I returned to bottle No. 1 and poured a more generous measure than I'd received the first time—right up to the top, indeed, of the thimble-like glass—and threw it down. A sip never seems to me to have any kind of taste at all. After contemplating the result of the larger glass I made a note on my score-card—'Not bad'.

It seemed, then, a slack definition, one of insufficient precision to isolate bottle No. 1 from the other eleven still to come. I filled my testing glass again to the brim and threw it down. This wine was beginning to grow on me. It seemed to have more body, more suppleness than before. I made an additional note on my score-card—'plenty of body, v. supple'—and moved on to bottle No. 2.

While waiting to get hold of it I had two pieces of cheese, to clear the palate for the next delight, and then realized, having had an inadequate lunch, that I was rather hungry and so had two more pieces of cheese and four small biscuits. This hurried snack had the unfortunate effect of creating rather tacky conditions in the mouth which bottle No. 2, after three applications, did nothing to clear. I gave it a bad mark—'v. light and immature' —and moved on to bottle No. 3.

A Table Wine for Removing Grease

No. 3 certainly cleared away the cheese and biscuits, so I dallied with it for a while and then moved on, with a slight singing beginning in the ears, to bottle No. 4. By the time I'd finished with bottle No. 4 I found I'd forgotten to make a note about bottle No. 3 so I went back to it and browsed there for quite some time, unable to make up my mind about the bouquet, or indeed about anything else. A certain sameness of flavour seemed to be establishing itself.

By this time some of the other connoisseurs had completed the course and were being served with cool white wine in large glasses so I called a temporary halt to my own researches and had two of them, rather quickly, to neutralize the somewhat corrosive effect of a lot of red wine on a chilly evening before dinner. Quite a lot of red wine also seemed to have got on to my score-card, obliterating my comments on bottles No. 1 and 2.

Panic set in. Perhaps we had to hand in our score-cards and get marks for them! I was making a quick reassessment of bottles No. 1 and 2 with a glass in each hand when the management announced the result. The first four bottles—marking, incidentally, the limit of my inventory—were the nitric acid, all the rest were genuine Beaujolais.

I started eating cheese-and-biscuits very quickly indeed.

12

The Man of Steel, in Wax

DOES one rather have the feeling that one is loping along about three years behind one's leaders who, at this very moment now, are doing something for one's benefit or suppression which one may be lucky enough to hear about in approximately three years' time?

One uses 'one' in place of 'I', of course, to lend to a purely personal and possibly disordered fancy the weight of an opinion held by all cultured persons everywhere. Compare Mr. Tony Richardson, the stage and film director, in an interview last week: 'Basically, everything one feels has to be expressed through one's work—it's through one's work that one speaks most eloquently.'

One shall continue, therefore, in terms of one to speak of one's suddenly alarming certainty that the politicians and generals and scientists who lead the nations of the world are at this precise moment making decisions about courses of action which have to be kept secret not only from one but from everyone upon whose behalf these decisions have been made.

It's a feeling—smouldering for quite a while—which has been fanned into a blaze by publication of the rumour that the embalmed cadaver of Uncle Joe Stalin was, in fact, only Uncle Joe as far as the head and the hands were concerned and that all the rest was a wax model, possibly from GUM, intended for the display of middle-aged tractor drivers' overalls.

If this be true—and one does rather feel that one is entitled to believe it—it amounts to a confidence trick which one cannot help regarding as fearsomely typical of the leaders' attitude towards the led.

Breakfast, say, in the Kremlin one morning in 1955. Smoked sturgeon, borsch and a pot of vodka on the hob. All the serious boys gathered together, making decisions, when Dr. Alexis Prophylaxis is shown in, looking as pale as though he, too, had been under glass for two years.

He has bad news about Comrade Lenin's companion in the tomb. Is it safe to mention the name? At any rate, if it could be put this way, he's looking in rather poor shape. Grovelling apologies from the Doctor. Not entirely his fault but if a full and frank confession is required, in public, only too glad to oblige, with the proviso that after justice has been done he would prefer to be cremated rather than embalmed——

These babblings are cut short by the serious boys, who swiftly devise the wax model ruse and tell Prophylaxis to get on with it. The Doctor, a reversionist old Bolshevik, is appalled. All those millions of people filing through the tomb, doing homage to a wax model intended for the display of middle-aged tractor drivers'——

The voice comes from on high. 'They're not going to know about it. Get on.'

There's a feeling in the air these days that we, the led, scarcely know about anything. All those acres of American Air Force bases with bulldozers in the far distance tearing the tops off verdant English hills. Thin vapour trails miles up in the sky. Who is flying, and where to, and what for?

Atomic research stations in the wilds of Scotland. 'Keep out. Don't look. Go away.'

Mysterious couriers, agents, envoys hurrying through airports and into waiting planes, speaking to no one, met at the other end by long black cars, disappearing into the limbo from which they came. A vast, infinitely busy world of those in the know, with the rest of us merely getting in the way.

One has to allow that they do it very well. They preserve their secrets a treat. What does go on, for instance, in that fortress in the Mall, apart from that rather attractive creeper gaining a firmer and firmer grip on it year by year? What was all that, some years ago, about a colossal underground barracks somewhere near Tottenham Court Road? Is it true that the whole of Daws Hill, near High Wycombe, has been hollowed out by the Americans and that there is an hydraulically operated lid on top which can be opened up to let something fearful out?

One simply doesn't know. Loping along three years behind the event, one hears rumours, but by the time they arrive, of course, they're out of date, and the leaders of the world are being secretive about something else.

It suits me, for one. I'm easy. Like everyone else, I've got quite enough to do preserving my own secrets—Inland Revenue returns, movements last night, etc.—to have any really serious concern about what the boys on top are trying to conceal from me.

13

Dem Bones, dem Bones, dem Grey Bones

AFTER a while the trot round the corner with the Red Riding Hood basket to the supermarket, shuffling about in their deep freeze and coming up with yet another pre-cleaned, pre-cooked, pre-carved, gaily packaged little television supper—merely heat and eat—promotes, particularly in the absence of a television set, a feeling of over-dependence on the enfeebling facilities of the modern world.

At a headlong pace, words tripping over themselves, I rush to state that deep-frozen, pre-cooked, gaily packaged little television suppers are beyond question the reverse of being *physically* enfeebling, packed as they are from colour picture on the front to simple instructions on the back with nut-brown goodness, vitamin-wise 100 per cent glutamate pure. The enfeeblement is to the spirit, the sensation of the loss of the manliness that sent the cavemen, with a club, on the track of dinosaur giblet minestrone with noodles, dinner gained by work, courage and imagination, nutriment torn from nature by the sweat of the simian brow.

The memory returned of an Aran Island legend, wherein Pat Mullen, the Man of Aran himself, resolved to settle his commissariat problems by cooking, at one blow, enough stew to last him for three months and to this end he furbished up a forty-gallon oil-drum and set it upon a great turf fire and all the people of Aran came to their king with pigs and sheep, some of them skinned, and ducks and hens and threw them in tribute into the mighty pot and bushels of potatoes and onions and cabbages went in and for a week there was great drinking and singing while the cauldron bubbled, and for good measure at the end the

King tossed in a boulder-sized lump of rock-salt, and when the ceremonial tasting came the enormous stew was that powerful they had to take it out into the middle of Galway Bay in a hooker and drop it into the deep. . . .

A more continental type of stew, I calculated, going easy on the rock-salt, wool and feathers, might well serve to get me off the little telly suppers and back among the men who struggled for their food.

Big saucepans, suitable for big stews, turned out to be prohibitively expensive. It was as though there were a tax on size in cooking, as though it were a threat to the nation's food resources for a man to require a saucepan large enough to hold a cow's leg and a stone of mixed vegetables. I got one in the end, not very large, for 28s. 11d., after dodging pots retailing at anything up to a fiver, even if they did have non-stick, aluminiumized, even-heat-distributive bottoms.

The butcher was interesting on the subject of meat for stews. He said he wished he'd been on the 'Panorama' programme when Dimbleby was doing the butchers. He'd have told him a thing or two. 'Everyone's gone crackers,' the butcher said, itemizing one of the things he would have told Dimbleby, 'buying fillet steak for stewing. Natural they think the price of meat is high.' I came out with a heap of fragments at 4s. 6d. a pound and fippence wortha bones—a huge, glistening, blue-white knuckle and a chopped-up shank as long and as thick as your arm.

The preliminary stages of the manufacture of stock were alarming. The boiling of the beautiful blue-white knuckle and the pinkish, ivory shank threw up a fearful, mud-coloured scum. It was as though, in pursuance of the haute cuisine of the Aran Islands, I'd thrown a ton of murphies straight into the pot out of the sod. At the end of two hours of low simmering the glistening bones were grey and muddy themselves, seeming to threaten anthrax or foot-and-mouth disease. Straining was obviously required, and here, failing a strainer, the first, amateurish improvisation broke out. A glazed, brown coffee-pot with a filtering device. The stock stuck in the filter, but with a toothpick to clear the filter holes I managed to get quite a lot of it into the coffee-pot, somewhat grey still in colour but looking more anthrax-free. I wrapped the boiling bones in newspaper and put them in the dustbin, feeling like Hare acting under the orders of Burke, scoured the saucepan and filled it with stock from the coffee-pot in four strained helpings. Coming out of the spout, it looked like a lot of coffee I've seen in various places.

Ready to go now, a great, nourishing, self-made, simmering melange of meat, potatoes, leeks, carrots, onions, substantial clove of garlic and herbs sounding like a society wedding— Rosemary Thyme and Basil Fennel. It bubbled and fennelled away all day, filling the residency with the scents and sounds of a factory ship in attendance upon a whaling fleet.

I dined upon it, in it, off it, in solo state at the fashionable hour of 7.45 that night and even after four helpings, decreasing admittedly in size, made gratifyingly little impression on the basic mass. Indeed, the surrounding soup, or stock, was by now so rich that it could have endured 100 per cent dilution and retained every shred of its identity. Little telly suppers, it was plain, would not be required for a long, long time.

A new problem, however, by now has become apparent. Running a big, permanent stew is like owning a big, permanent dog. That is, you've got to keep it exercised. You can't go out and leave it or it pines, goes sick. For the last three days I've been too busy to give my stew a run. It looks bad, and probably is.

Failing Galway Bay, I may have to sink the whole suffocating saucepan in the Serpentine.

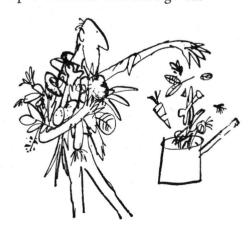

14

Hands, Legs and Writer's Face

IN THE stable, respectful, good old days before the camera became candid and the public didn't know it wanted to see at least the back teeth—failing the basic psyche—of the sitter, photographs suitable for inclusion in the elegant magazines were a matter of one rigid, non-breathing studio pose and thank you so much, charming, charming, that will be quite all.

Actresses were glorified with a halo of heavenly light behind the hair, whatever might be the nature of their private lives. Officers and gentlemen squared up to the tripod like men, staring coldly at the centre of the lens in the position of attention, even while sitting down. Actors appeared in sculptured profile, with a finger laid along the line of the jaw, indicating intelligence while concealing structural deficiencies. Authors had pipes, often provided by the studio, clenched in a firm hand at a safe distance from the face, demonstrating profundity of mind. Duchesses looked ducal, politicians sternly benevolent and all children like models for Bubbles.

In those stable, respectful, good old days photographers approached their clients like reassuring, kindly dentists, intent upon producing by purring words and soothing gestures a condition of general anaesthesia in which their work might be swiftly and painlessly completed before the clients regained consciousness and looked like their old—very old—selves again.

Nowadays, having one's picture taken for inclusion in an elegant magazine bears a fair resemblance to being involved in a fast, cross-talk variety act, coupled with Judo postures, where both performers are on the verge of a nervous breakdown. I was done only the other day and am still sufficiently strung up

48

to be chattering volubly, smiling wolfishly, laughing merrily, pointing imperiously, scratching industriously and crouching in corners in craven fear.

The invitation came from an elegant magazine who wanted my views on Christmas—enough to turn the heart to stone—with a photograph to illuminate and personalize whatever these views might be. Views to antagonize neither Church, State nor People—delicate matter, Christmas—were run together and inserted into the phone and an hour later the photographer arrived, in something of a hurry to get on and do Lady Lewisham, whose reflections were also required upon the Feast.

I had, arranged for him in a good light, typewriter, pipe and the rudiments of Writer's Face, but we scrapped these archaic props instantly and went out, with a kitchen chair, into the cold and shadowy backyard. We put the chair beside a drainpipe. 'Just sit on the edge of it,' the photographer said, 'throw out your legs, lounge about and keep talking.'

He was fixing the sights on a short, blunt, huge-barrelled death-ray gun, a camera of a sort I'd never seen before, but then all good photographers these days are Leonardos, simultaneously scientists, artists, psychologists, engineers, even prospectors, digging for the basic psyche through the living rock.

I got up as much basic psyche as I could, nearly divided in half by the edge of the kitchen chair, while the photographer ducked and weaved around me, firing his death-ray from all angles at the range of three feet. Conversation, staccato but very full, had shifted up a notch from the weather to the discovery and character analysis of mutual friends. And all the time the death-ray clicking on. The output of vitality was so great that it was impossible not to slacken off while he reloaded. He came back on target. 'Lounge a bit more—relax—laugh . . .' Hard down on the accelerator once more.

Wild cachinnation, eyes rolling, blinking, occluding, head writhing, teeth protruding and receding, all becoming more and more extravagant in the desire to propitiate the huge and

D   49

hungry muzzle of the gun. The photographer, who'd been questioning, provoking, encouraging in the interests of his art, stopped to reload once more. 'I suppose,' he said, 'you couldn't use your hands a bit?'

We took another reel, with hands. One hand clutching the forehead, both hands pulling like bell-ropes on the ears, one hand round the back of the neck, the other covering an eye. Then we disengaged from the face and the hands pointed to the wall, to the sky, to the drainpipe. They flapped like bats, the digits stuck up like palisades then hooked together in rigor mortis and all the time gabble-gabble, laugh-laugh, being naturally relaxed and animated for the gun.

At the end of that reel the photographer said he hadn't quite got the one he wanted yet. 'Try it this way.' Subject and photographer were suddenly crouched on all fours, face to face, the subject waving its front paws and by now nearly barking like a dog. . . .

After he'd gone I couldn't help wondering if he was applying the same deep-drilling technique to Lady Lewisham, but decided against it.

With some fortunate, naturally mobile subjects the basic probably comes out perfectly sweetly and smoothly, with no greater stimulus than a faint halo of light behind the hair.

15

A Covering for Carlessness

SUDDENLY, carlessness sets in—a state as unnatural, as tumbling to the wits as weightlessness. Worse, more painful, having affiliations with the amputation of a leg.

Movement from place to place becomes a matter of intricate, advance planning. Strict punctuality—a personal pleasure—becomes the plaything of chance. If three required buses sweep past in convoy does it mean that half an hour will go by before three more appear, going even faster past the request stop? If half an hour extra is allowed for the travelling time does this ensure that one required bus will instantly halt at the request stop, delivering the traveller at his destination half an hour too soon?

Is there currency of the right amount in hand? Sixpence and a pound note means walking half a mile to the beginning, when one is launched upon an eightpenny ride, of the sixpenny stage. A total of only four shillings in the reticule means that it's absolutely impossible to travel by taxi anywhere.

And yet these first few weeks of carlessness can easily be identified as the good old days. It has not been raining. That is, it has been possible to walk to and wait at bus-stops and come out socially acceptable—in the sense of not having apparently fallen into the canal—at the other end. But what will happen, when the winter rains set in in earnest, to the carless person who has neither overcoat nor mackintosh but, self-destructively, in their place a pathological loathing of all overcoats and mackintoshes in their present form?

I'd like to get mackintoshes out of the way first, because I really want to kick the lining out of overcoats. Mackintoshes come semi-military—epaulettes, mile-wide, cross-over storm collars, mad, brass rings (for bayonets, grenades, water-bottles?) on the belt, loops, gussets, paraphernalia everywhere, twenty minutes to get into and have to be cut off when wet. Or they're semi-hunting, flat, hard with enough room in the skirt to accommodate a horse, made of material which absorbs urban dirt like a sponge. Or Italian, three-quarter-length white paper, through which the Nordic winds skewer the very soul. . . .

Put the macs back on the rack, Jack.

But OVERCOATS. Old Billy Boaconstrictor, the Iron Maiden herself. A trim, navy-blue, Melton overcoat with half-belt, velvet collar facings, v. smart. On the top of what is that going to go? A v. smart, gent's business suiting. Furthermore, it's got to be surmounted by a hat and balanced on either side by gloves and a bamboo-handled umbrella, and it needs a lean, business face and somewhere respectable to go. Out.

Casually belted camel-hair? Prohibitively expensive, if genuine, and crippling, dry-cleaner's overheads, coupled with the appearance of a Brighton bookmaker only two losing favourites ahead of the police. Right out.

Single-breasted, leather-buttoned, raglan-shouldered, grouse-shooter's drooper, with large patch-pockets suitable for the transport of deceased hares? Slip into Nellie's Club at the back of Berwick Market in one of those and the clientele would instantly assume themselves to be in the presence of a plain-clothes man, unobtrusively mingling with his surroundings, and start mangling. . . .

Overcoats loosen my mind. I've made terrible mistakes with overcoats, looking for the one which can be thrown on and forgotten, over any kind of clothes, not crying out for a hat or spats or other supporters, just a rather elegant, in a slightly Bohemian way, wind-proof, rain-repellent *covering*, really, with a collar which can be permanently turned up without looking like Sir Francis Drake's Sunday ruff.

My last overcoat found a very suitable grave a year ago. A

fearful thing. Three-quarter length, camel-hair type, sporting motorist category, about a size too small, with pockets suitable for the transport of one spark-plug or a mag spanner. It was nicked—God bless 'im—by someone in the pub in Covent Garden at seven o'clock in the morning while I was engaged in theological discussion with Mr. Mick Mulligan, the distinguished band-leader, never to be seen again.

The one before that was worse. A duffel-coat with the hood turned into a leather-bound, *Oberstgrüppenführer's* storm collar. Someone mercifully left it lying across a double-filament electric fire. The one before that was my own invention. Brown herringbone, no buttons, no buckle on the belt. No wear, after the first fitting.

An umbrella—solo, of course—might well be the answer to the whole thing. By solo I mean not as an adjunct to a trim, half-belted Melton but an umbrella out—up—on its own. An enormous golf umbrella, big enough to live inside and have visitors. Blue and white candy-striped, or perhaps even in the personal, national colours of green, white and yellow?

An even better idea! An umbrella in a neutral shade of beige or terra-cotta, upon which various firms could buy advertising space, like the mini-cabs. . . .

There's one thing to be said for the state of carlessness. It may soak the socks but it certainly sharpens the mind.

16

The Umbrella Men

THE interest attendant upon self-instruction in the basic technique of running one, coupled with a perception of the artistic potentialities of advanced handling, have gone some way towards compensating me for the purchase of an umbrella which after only two days—one of them dry—already looks like a stage property employed twice-nightly in a comedy routine by the late Nellie Wallace.

In the buying of this foul, animated black bag, swanking, ignorance and parsimony met with their full and just reward.

Hurrying into this strip-lit, pickled oak, art-bamboo gentlemen's haberdashers and rattling out the request, 'Umbrella, anything will do, sure to leave it in a taxi,' I was trying to make one thing very clear, and to conceal several others.

The thing I was trying to make clear was that umbrella buying to me was as frequent and as trivial an occurrence as the purchase of a box of matches. Among the things I was trying to conceal was the fact that I wanted the cheapest one in the shop, that I had no knowledge at all of what umbrellas cost and that even by making a minute examination of umbrellas, both open and closed, I would be unable to tell whether they were good, bad or rotten. In the present-day technological world, where everyone is an expert on something, not to know anything about something amounts to an admission of mental deficiency, and this—impelled by the normal, revolting motives of vanity and arrogance—I wished to avoid.

Combined, all these absurdities led to my buying, very quickly, an umbrella for two guineas, a shattering charge for a contrivance of black cotton, wire and a yellow cane handle, daubed here and there with touches of dark-oak stain to make it look, presumably, jungle-weathered. The fundamental reason for my selection of this gimcrack horror was that the next, slightly better, umbrella was exactly twice as much, and also, of course, the fact that it was raining.

In repose, and viewed at a distance through half-closed eyes, the umbrella looked very like one of those slim, silky-steel rapiers carried at the trail by Guards officers bowler-hatting off duty. Open, receiving its baptism of rain and viewed in close-up from underneath, it looked exactly like a stage property employed in a comedy routine by the lady already mentioned.

The perimeter of the sack hung in scallops between the points of the ribs, while the span or dome of the whole thing was no larger than a gnome's toadstool. The shaft, shank or main chassis member protruding skinnily from the imitation-massive, jungle-type handle was the thickness of a knitting needle of a bore suitable for the tatting of an unweaned baby's Angora wool bootee. It terminated in a pin-like, wholly feminine parasol ferrule. Also, one of the seams had already split to the length of an inch, so that rain dripped through.

I decided, however, to retain this flotsam of the umbrella-maker's art in view of the fact that to return it to the haberdasher could lead only to the purchase of the four-guinea instrument, but I do have to allow that while it's only semi-effective against rain it has provided me, in its rolled condition, with the opportunity to get the physical feel of a number of personalities up till now foreign to my own.

An oaken settle in a public house, for instance, with the knees widespread, bread-basket advanced, right arm extended and the hand placed firmly on the crook of the umbrella, its ferrule planted solidly on the floor, creates a Chestertonian aura—a man of presence, a man not to be shifted from his opinions but, withal, a well-spread, generous man, one ready to receive, to digest, to reflect with wit and wisdom upon the news and views of the world. There's a rotundity about this personality, fortified by its umbrella. It's a personality that stays itself with stoops of ale.

In delightful contradistinction is the lean cavalryman, good leg for a boot, all bone and whipcord, who strides down the street giving not a jot for unmounted civilians and their pettifogging, prudent little ways. A cossack, a centaur, an adventurer, he grips his umbrella down near the ferrule, with a harsh, horse-laugh for convention, and cracks the handle from time to time against the sinewy, stirrup-hardened muscles of his calf. And from this, in a flash, by releasing the elastic band, letting the black, bedraggled wings of the umbrella hang lumpily out, plod plod down the street, back humped, ferrule tapping, mumbling to himself—the old, mad inventor with the secret of perpetual motion that no one wants to know. . . .

A caste of thousands, created by a single umbrella. Versatility of a scope to cause communal mouth-watering among the knights Olivier and Guinness, and Lon Chaney's ghost. And yet, despite all this richness, there is one type of part I cannot play. The mysterious, steel-jawed stranger in the trenchcoat, the First, Second, Third Man (?), standing sentinel in the alleyway. It starts to rain. He puts up his umbrella—and there's that ludicrous gnome's toadstool, with the scalloped perimeter and the baby's bootee knitting needle up the middle, and all we're short of now is a comic song.

17

A Scuffle in the Sac de Bousculade

THE gentleman of style, before departing for the Riviera, spends many thoughtful hours of trial and error amid the Italian-American haberdashery of Shaftesbury Avenue, fingering the linen-nylon tapered trouserings, the beach-shirts with the pineapple or other tropical motif, light-weight jackets with reversible shawl collars for the cocktail hour, casual moccasins for promenading, intricate sandals for the *plage*, straw jockey caps and boaters and then, two days later, he's strolling about Cap Ferrat, Beaulieu or St. Tropez wearing, if he has any sense, a pair of shorts and five shillings' worth of rope-soled *espadrilles*.

The Italian-American haberdashery lies in his suitcase at the hotel or villa, undisturbed save for the nesting activities of ants. What appeared to be garments of gossamer texture in the heat of the London summer turn out to be the equivalents of chain-mail in the furnace of the Côte d'Azur.

So here is this previously well-dressed gentleman, free of all restraint or inhibition in his scruffy shorts and canvas slippers, and the only cloud on his azure-blue horizon is the fact that every time he sits down, or stands up, everything, including his passport, travellers' cheques, cigarette lighter and loose change, falls out of his pockets, for the reason that shorts are not constructed for the secretion and transport of urban paraphernalia. So this man, previously free of all restraint and inhibition, walks about clutching both his side pockets while urging friends bringing up the rear to keep an eye on his passport in the pocket on his hip. Sitting down, or standing up, involves making a complete inventory of all possessions. The taking out of a handkerchief can divide one's capital in half. Small French children are as quick as the next at getting their little feet on top of rolling, loose change.

Happily, there is a solution to this torment. What every sensible man will be wearing on the Riviera this season, shortly after he reads this, will be *un sac de bousculade*, or scuffle-bag. I could even come right out into the open and say that it's a hand-bag for men. Rather a lot of bags are creeping into this exposition, but I find that a large, zippered sponge-bag makes the best scuffle-bag because even the *avant garde* boutiques of the Riviera are not as yet making male handbags, though of course they will be on sale everywhere from Menton to Marseille before the end of the week.

My own *sac de bousculade* now contains my passport, travellers' cheques, a scissors, a purse, a bottle of vitamin pills, two pipes, a tobacco pouch, a cigarette lighter, a packet of pipe-lighters, a handkerchief, a noggin of cognac, a comb, a small notebook, a penknife and a pair of bathing-trunks and even at that, as a *sac de bousculade*, it's only in its infancy. *Le bon Dieu seul* knows what else will be in it by the time I leave here at the end of the month.

The original invention of this daring reticule must be credited to an Englishman who some years ago, lost to all sense of con-science and duty, sold up everything he didn't want in England to buy everything he did want in Villefranche, like a motor-cruiser, a villa, wine at 2*s*. 6*d*. per bottle, total idleness and absolute peace of mind. He took to a sponge-bag for his acces-sories after finding that the pockets of shorts distributed an almost continuous stream of currency over the side of the cruiser, a matter of special irritation to him as it was absolutely the only flaw in his indolent, disgraceful and glorious way of life. He referred to it, however, only as 'my little bag'. It was I—and I want it to be remembered in the form of a percentage when full production gets under way—who gave it the name of scuffle-bag, or *sac de bousculade*, and simultaneously invented a new Riviera divertissement, not an easy thing to do on this pleasure-crazed coast. It is, simply, to *bousculer*, or to get right head-down into your sponge-bag and have a really good scuffle around. The thrill of discovery, the contrapuntal chinking of pills and keys and fountain pens and money add up to hours of deeply satisfying pleasure in the cafés or on the beach. If one is fortunate enough to meet a fellow *bousculadier* it is also possible to enjoy a *jeu de bousculade*, challenging him to match your bric-á-brac piece by piece, and scoring a point if he cannot do so. To this end I've just added an ashtray to my *sac*.

One word of warning to novice *bousculadiers* coming fresh to their work. Do learn the French for, 'My faith, gendarme, someone's knocked off my scuffle-bag and it's left me completely up the spout!'

It will, almost certainly, come in useful.

18

Up with the Owls

IN THE jolly communism of holiday-villa life it is necessary for all of us to behave with the strictest regard for the little quirks and foibles, the likes and dislikes, the temperamental delicacies, the howling, uncontrollable neuroses of our merry companions, because otherwise much pleasure time will be spent in reading the English newspapers in separate corners of the garden, in silence so deeply injured that it drowns even the deafening roar of traffic along the Corniche Inférieur a thousand feet below.

When, therefore, I rise perfectly naturally at 4.30 every morning to be ready, washed, shaved and bed neatly made, to greet the molten sun as it shoots over the mountain at 6.18, my own delicacy of temperament causes me to pad about the villa like a mouse wearing velvet slippers—two pairs—for the reason that the others regard even a 10 a.m. reveille as an assault upon the senses so brutal as to deprive them of the power of coherent thought for the remainder of the day.

Like all holiday villas, however, this one is constructed in such a way that it renders noiseless padding about, washing, shaving and bed-making a virtual impossibility, so that I'm driven to adopt a series of noise-dampening devices so pettifoggingly complex that there are times, I have to confess, when I feel like dropping the garbage can off the roof on to the concrete patio and getting those hog-like slobs up and out of it, so that they, too, can enjoy the golden, shimmering beauty of the Riviera dawn.

The bathroom is a windowless, airless cupboard wedged between the main bedroom and the kitchen, with what appear to be cardboard doors leading into each. This has the effect of turning the bathroom into a kind of echo-chamber, with the doors acting as loudspeakers for the fortissimo projection, in high fidelity, of sounds made within which would otherwise be inaudible to a bat.

Tooth-cleaning, for instance, is magnified into the uproar of a pebble-dash wall being scrubbed in a frenzy of rage by a giant with a fifty-foot yardbrush. The water-heater sounds like a jet-engined bomber, engine-testing in a cave in the Cheddar Gorge. Operation of the cistern blends Niagara with the Last Trump. So the bathroom is out for ablutions, and so, too, is the kitchen. The hot-water tap starts off the water-heater-bomber again, while the cold one shuts down with a sharp, staccato series of clonks sufficiently vicious to loosen plaster from the ceiling. So what I do is to save a small, plastic bucket of water from the night before and wash, at 4.35 a.m., in a low stone shed filled with old newspapers and cardboard boxes in which are domiciled lizards, ants, crickets and other flying accelerators, to hasten a process which is pretty perfunctory in any case.

Shaving, however, has to be brought closer to the house, as it is necessary to plug an electric razor into a point in the sitting-room which I share as a boudoir with a sixteen-year-old lad who does more solid ear-pounding than anyone I've ever seen. Indeed, I often feel he's missing so much of the dawn that I've been tempted to drop the garbage can on the tiled floor right beside his little basket, to see if that would help him up except that I'm pretty certain it would merely wake everyone else while leaving the lad undisturbed.

The electric razor, then, is placed on a cushion on a chair on the patio with another cushion on top of it, and the flex is led under the door to the point in the sitting-room. Plug in, the low hum starts, spring out silently closing two glass doors and two shutters and then shave at the full stretch of the flex, trying to keep the noise as far away as possible. Coughing, sneezing, liver attacks, the staggers and other morning inevitables have to be taken right down the road into a small clump of olive trees, and muted even there. After a couple of hours of this tensely inhibited work I find the folding and tidying of a newspaper nearly splits the ear-drums.

A curious thing happened, though, the other morning. An early start had been planned to the day. Breakfast, they said, about six, so that we could get through Nice before the traffic really began.

I had the breakfast table noisily laid by 5.30, dropping a lot of knives and forks. I played the yardbrush scrubbing for them, the jet-bomber engine-testing and Niagara and the Last Trump—twice. I coughed, staggered about and put the electric razor into a saucepan for extra resonance.

Not a stir. Not a cheep. When eventually I did wake them by pounding with both fists on the bedroom door at 6.15 they said it wasn't worth going at all, now that I'd left it so late.

19

The Beautiful Brown People

WHILE the rain lashes down on Manchester and sleet follows hail into Bradford and gales of bitter wind turn the thoughts of the people of St. Albans, without cheer, towards Christmas the Mediterranean remains purple-blue and mirror calm, save where the bow of the yacht churns it into frothy cream.

On the after-deck a bronzed yachtsman takes his ease in a deep basket-chair, smoking a small but good cigar. Three miles inshore the roaring buses, the bellowing lorries, the hooting cars, the snarling scooters turn the waterfront of Nice into a full-scale representation of the Inferno. Out here, on the purple-blue sea, there is only the gentle murmur of the diesel engines and the soft swishing of the waves.

And yet the bronzed yachtsman is not content. Something is missing in his paradise. It's eleven o'clock in the morning, and what would be nice would be a glass of very cold champagne.

The yachtsman makes the effort. A quarter-turn of the head to the right, the articulation of words. 'Press the bell, will you, and tell Hans—champagne . . .' The voice trails away. The effort has been too great. It's a comfort to the yachtsman to know that a glass of bubbly, very cold, will shortly be placed in his hand. It's also a comfort to the yachtsman to know that the chef is even now preparing lunch in the galley and that the skipper will soon be stopping the yacht and the deck-hands will place a ladder over the side so that bathing can take place in the wine-dark, soup-hot sea and tonight we'll be in San Remo with the speed-boat standing by to return us to real baths and real beds, lying to an anchor outside the minimal noises and disturbances of the harbour.

And yet a vigorous young man, retired at forty with a yacht even bigger than this one, observed to me the other evening that he wasn't sure about the benefits to the soul of lotus-eating afloat on the Mediterranean. He had a hankering, he said, to return to his estate in Yorkshire, and get down to some really serious farming, because after all you've got to make something of your life.

The mind, slackened off almost to nothing by a diet of pure lotus for the last four days, cannot come to grips with a proposition of such extraordinary complexity. What more, for instance, could one make of one's life than to be leaning over the rail as the yacht comes in the cool of the evening into a pine-fringed bay, on an island three hours out from St. Tropez, and there to greet us, in a rubber dinghy powered by an outboard motor, is a small party of female nudists from the colony at Lavant, all looking bronzed and fit and in merry mood?

The anchor goes down with a roar into sixty feet of water so clear that it's possible to read the time on a clock which is, curiously enough, resting on the silver sand below. It's the right place to keep time, too. We certainly don't want it up here.

And then, as darkness falls and a full, red moon arises, yachts converge upon our little bay from all points of the compass. The anchor chains rattle down, and the most extraordinary water-party begins. We have, it seems, hit by chance upon the rendez-vous of the *jeunesse dorée* of St. Tropez. Music comes across the black velvet water. All the yachts are lit up. Beautiful brown people are dancing on the decks. The naturists from Lavant are right in the middle of it all. Then, out of sheer joy, out of pure physical delight, all the yachts begin to sound their sirens, fog-horns and ships' bells. The little wooded bay echoes with grunt-ings and honkings and hootings and every kind of tintinnabula-tion. It's like the mating calls of unimaginable prehistoric monsters, snorting and gambolling in delight. And suddenly, then, piercing right through all this glorious, entirely beneficial pagan pleasure, comes an English voice, awesomely magnified by a loud-hailer from a big yacht anchored exclusively out near the point. It brings with it rain from Manchester and sleet from Oswestry and a cold, bitter wind from the Fens. It also brings with it conscience and duty and the need to make something, I mean let's face it, of your life.

'I say there, chaps,' the loud-hailer bawls, 'pack it up there, will you—Mother can't sleep!'

Filled with lotus leaves, and hungry for more and more and more, I am delighted to hear the beautiful brown people fall silent for a moment, and then reply to conscience and duty and rain and bitter winds with the biggest raspberry I have ever heard.

20

By Holiday Revived

PALLID, lean, eager, the whole nervous system tuned squeaking to high-C, the normal working pitch, they spare us a moment in their rush from meeting to conference, from conference to business lunch, from business lunch to special committee, from special committee to commercial cocktails, before galloping on to dinner and the clinching of the deal—pallid, lean, eager, all those fortunate ones who served their holiday time on the bitter, windswept beaches of Great Britain.

We, the slow, brown, plump ones, the mentally retarded children of the sun, still clinging to our Riviera clothes, physically, revolted by the hairy clutch of socks and shirts and ties and braces start with what speed our somnolent reflexes allow as the lean people shout greetings into our golden, half-closed ears.

'What *about* that tan! Lucky you—fighting fit, eh? Give you a buzz at nine tomorrow morning! Big things in store!'

They're gone, eyes glittering, muscles knotted in the cheek, minds whining like dynamos, to fling themselves into new enterprises, big autumn drives, brisk preparations involving cards printed and sent off in good time for Christmas. They're gone, speeding into the distance like tracer bullets, these lean, lucky ones tuned to the normal working pitch of high-C by a holiday in Britain so damp and so chilly that the bleak dark-oak portals of the office are as welcome, as bountifully nourishing to the soul, as the pearly gates of Heaven.

We, the slow, brown, fat ones, meditatively—like cows in mastication—scratching our mosquito souvenirs, sink to the backs of our necks again in our armchairs, making believe we feel beneath us still the hot, burning stones of the Côte d'Azur.

Before we can engage in big, new enterprises, business lunches, commercial cocktails, brisk preparations for the early dispatch of Christmas cards, an immense amount of personal work has to be done. A readying, as it were, for the autumn drive, a clearing of the decks, a sifting of the old to see what benefit any part of it might be to the new.

It's impossible, in our present golden somnolence, to give priority to any of the multitudinous personal tasks that lie ahead or even to estimate when work upon them might begin, but it will be undoubtedly interesting to see, for instance, if the bottle of *vin ordinaire*, purchased for 2s. 9d. in the little *alimentation* at the bottom of the hill, has survived the buffeting and jostling, the boiling and the refrigeration of a thousand miles in the boot of a car. If it has one plan for the autumn drive might be to hurry back to the little *alimentation* at the bottom of the hill and get some more, followed conceivably by the decision to remain *in situ*, and drink it there.

The bottle of wine lies, however, at the bottom of a bag filled either with London clothes that were never worn, or with Riviera clothes that were worn to rags and never washed, the whole presenting a problem in laundry and dry-cleaning of fathomless complexity. If, for example, the three London shirts which were never worn but which are undeniably crumpled go to the laundry it will make it impossible for me, shirtless, to play any part in the London commercial scene until their return. Would the act of wearing them remove some of the wrinkles? Does it, fundamentally, matter if a man's shirt is crumpled, provided that he is engaged upon a sufficiently big autumn deal? Speculation upon these imponderables proves so wearingly fruitless that I turn my mind, with even less eagerness, to the matter of the Riviera rags.

Would it not be wise to put them in the dustbin, to have done with memories, to annihilate nostalgia, to get back into socks and shirts and ties and braces and bite on the woolly bullet? Or have them laundered and dry-cleaned? Then, during the winter months, with central heating and electric fires and convector oil-heaters at full, radiant blast, slip them on and lie on the cold carpet, squeezing the ear-drums to hear the Mediterranean's baby, blue waves. . . .

Laundry and dry-cleaning and shorts and shirts get into a tangle so debilitating that I'm almost glad to find the crisis of rapidly fading sun-tan swimming slowly to the surface of the glassy-calm mind.

There's one thing to be said for Northern climes. Southern sun-tan shows up mahogany-dark in gloomy London mirrors. The protected areas shine out, by contrast, an incredibly icy white, providing deeply satisfying evidence of all the good work that has been done. After ten minutes of careful inspection in the full-length mirror behind the wardrobe door I come to the conclusion, however, that the contrast is not nearly as marked as it was, say, yesterday. In another week will everything, once again, be potato-grey? Should a sun-ray lamp be purchased? Would it create the same effect? How much are they? Is it a fact that without dark glasses they tend to strike you stone-blind?

Exhausted by such tightly knit conjectures, and finding myself in the bedroom, I lie down on the bed. It's 10.30 a.m.

Siesta time.

21

The Outsizer, Outside

WHATEVER Colin Wilson had to say about it—and it's all so long ago I cannot clearly remember his message—I'd rather be an Outsider than an Outsize.

What was the matter with the Outsider? Something about a man agonizingly aware of the chaos underlying the order in which most of his fellow men believe?

That's only a fleeting attack of the jigs in comparison with the screaming, bulging meemies that descend upon the Outsizer, when he's having a day on which he finds himself to be twice the size of *all* his fellow men, and particularly women. Fellow women? Get on.

One of these days started for me with trying to buy a pair of shoes.

At no time in the history of the world have men's feet had a wider choice of pouch. There are winkle-pickers and spade toes, moccasins and loafers, two-tie-wing-tips, bronze Cordovans, Mexican huarachas, Italian casuals, even elastic-sided, ecclesiastical chukka boots, presumably for clerics who wish to play polo, but they're only made for men—and clerics—with feet the size of ants. So, at least, it seems to the Outsizer, putting in a request for a moccasin-type, reversed-calf casual with concealed elastic gussets in Size Twelve E or, failing that, anything equally casual that will fit.

Nine shoe shops in a row—*nine*—and small, ant-footed assistants coming from every corner to gaze, shuddering, at the great, sad plates, curled and gnarled, overflowing the edges of the fitting-stools. 'No, no—nothing at all, nothing in sports or casual wear, not in that size, no demand, you see. . . .'

'Have you any other kind of boot, shoe, pouch, holster or other leather artifact that would contain these feet?'

They produce a pair of black, square-toed things with brass eyelets which D. H. Lawrence's father might conceivably have worn while attending Sunday service in a colliery town in 1852, or whenever it was. No bronze Cordovans, no huarachas. The Outsizer is out, cut off by his monstrous dogs from any part of the fashionable, moccasin-casual life of the ant-feet, dancing along the Promenade des Anglais in their Northampton *espadrilles*.

Feeling like Frankenstein, I clumped away, the great plates slapping on the echoing pavements, to make a purchase—half of lard and a tin of pepper—in a small, general store. It was Outsizer day, all right. The store seemed smaller than ever, and it was filled with tiny women. The proprietress's chin appeared to rest on the counter. A minute, female shopper backed away from beneath my elbow. Three more huddled in a corner beside the potted meats, gazing up in dread. I'm six feet five and nearly always have been, but now on Outsizer day I'd clearly got bigger. It was as though King Kong had lurched in, casting a monstrous shadow on the tiny scene. Total, breathless silence —the women looking for somewhere to run. It was then I found I'd lost the 10s. note set aside for the half of lard and the tin of pepper, tiny things in themselves.

Something prompted me to look out into the street, to see a woman four feet high pounce upon my note and stuff it into her shopping bag. I had to bend nearly double to shout into her ear, to establish ownership of the currency. The other midgets huddled more tightly together. King Kong was going berserk.

The size of a creature so vast in such close proximity scattered the note-whipper's natural acumen, and she gave it back. We re-entered the shop together, all the other midgets backing away. A moment later I pocketed the note-whipper's change, in mistake for my own. I felt fifty feet high, uncontrollable as a rogue gorilla. Bereft of all sense, I picked up the shopping basket belonging to the midget beside me and started out of the shop. Squeaks of outrage, as if from mice. I went back in again, gave the basket back to the wrong midget. In leaving, I stepped on the note-whipper's foot. I fled, round the corner, colossal, Brobding-nagian, bulging, sweating, and nearly trampled a little child to death, playing in the road. It was time to separate myself from miniscule humanity until this terrible Outsizer feeling passed away.

I went for a walk in the park, stepping delicately so as not to shake the trees. It's a curious park, silent and empty, fenced off into wide paths wandering through tangled undergrowth. A good place for giants, where they can do no harm.

The bird suddenly appeared in front of me, a baby bird too young to have a tail. It flopped about on the path, helpless on its stubby wings. Seeing the giant, it turned in tiny, heroic defiance, opening its beak in an inaudible yell. Holding my enormous breath, I shooed it back through the fence. The undergrowth looked vast, inviting, all-concealing, safe. The fence was low enough for me, a giant, to step over. 'Make room, bird,' I said, 'I'm coming in.' One leg raised, then a roar like the last Trump.

A park-keeper. 'Come back out of that! What you think you're doing? Git back on the path, like everybody else!'

Like everybody else? He didn't know he was talking to a man Outsize.

22

Something Fearful Down Below

THE great thing is to get out and about, to undertake enter-prises, to be ready without a moment of hesitation or counter-suggestion to go anywhere, do anything, if one is to suck on the full and infinitely variegated flavour of life.

Like the other evening, when someone asked if I would like to come and do some stripping in a club. I accepted immediately, out of interest, confident that if the scheduled disrobement began to tend in any way towards vulgarity or lack of taste a premature departure could be made on the ground of incipient bronchitis and doctor's orders, without loss of face or any other feature that might be currently involved.

A somewhat downbeat discovery on arrival. The stripping turned out to be the removal of paint from the wooden panelling in the club's dining-room, a voluntary effort on the part of a group of the members, to the number of three. They were already at work, scratching away in total absorption with their own private sections of moulding, panelling and window-frames.

The proprietress herself was also at work, in headscarf and seventh-best dress, covered with a dark-brown dust. She took a moment out to tell me that the lease of the club was about to terminate, and that the whole building might well be razed to the ground within a matter of months. It would, however, she observed, be nice to have the dining-room looking its best just before or, more probably, at the moment when the demoli-tion squad moved in. Pleased by the quixotry of it, I started to strip myself, only to find that the *mise en scène* had yet another and even more stimulating ingredient.

The bar in the room immediately below us had been hired

for a private party by the last man on earth I wished to see, a publisher who had been waiting for nearly a year for a 98 per cent revision of a work of which I'd lost my only copy nearly six months before. A crowded and unlikely juxtaposition, but one familiar to persons who take the trouble to get out and about.

The crash came an hour later, a reverberating roar from the room below that seemed to go on for several minutes. Something of immense weight had clearly fallen from a great height, something so large that it was impossible to estimate its nature or the effect that it had had upon a crowded room.

No clue came from below. All below, indeed, was silent as the grave. A moment before there had been the thump of a three-piece orchestra, the babble of literary conversation. Now there was only the silence of the grave.

It was interesting to note the reaction of the strippers. What we, including the proprietress, did was to go on stripping in total absorption with the task in hand. No one spoke. No one moved his eye from his moulding or panelling to catch even fleetingly the eye of his neighbour. I think I speak for all of us when I say that we felt that whatever had happened down below was too big to promote reaction. Screamings on our part, or rushings to the rescue, would have seemed a puny and inadequate response to the thunderous majesty of that fearful roar. We went on stripping, a little more conscientiously than before.

Suddenly, the barman from down below was amongst us. He waved his hands, trying to grasp words from the air. 'The ceiling!' The voice was falsetto. 'Huge lump. Everyone lying about. Bleeding . . .'

We went on stripping, but softly now, waiting for the proprietress's reaction. It was only briefly delayed. 'Oh yes?' she said, with a politely rising inflection. 'Well, there's nothing I can do about it, and I'm not properly dressed to go down.' She gave him a kindly, abstracted smile and returned to her work, as did, after a moment, the rest of us, with the refined air of persons too

73

delicately reared to have truck with the uncouth, coarse and strident common world.

It was very interesting indeed. The principle, stated loudly by our silence, seemed to be that persons conscientiously engaged in stripping paint off dining-room panels could not, of their nature, be expected to concern themselves with the vulgarity of bodies flattened by a falling ceiling, lying about bleeding in the bar below. The barman seemed to recognize the validity of it, and went away.

Things slid back into reality after that. The general bleeding turned out to be an exaggeration. Only one woman, in fact, had suffered a small cut on the back of her hand. The party below, however, ripe for continuing drama, sent for an ambulance, which took her away.

Watching her, I only just saved myself from falling out of the window. It would have been a very proper conclusion to an interesting evening out and about if I'd fallen, stripped to the buff, carrying with me a wrought-iron balcony and a window-box filled with geraniums, on the head of the publisher whom I'd been trying to avoid for a year.

23

And Peerenboom You, Too

THANKS are bursting out all over.

Twice, within the last few terrible weeks of fear and crisis, an American voice has been raised in public, to thank the British people for being what they are.

The first thanker went so far as to buy advertising space in a newspaper to express his gratitude for a wonderful visit. The second, more economically, wrote a letter to an editor, but then he had a lot more thanks to convey.

He wanted, for their friendliness, courtesy and helpfulness, to thank our police, bus and taxi drivers, store and restaurant clerks and all the people on the streets, and even then he had thanks left over for the Gordon Highlanders' dancers, the Grenadier Guards band and the sentries at Buckingham Palace, Horse Guards and Clarence House—the latter group for their patience and tolerance during the taking of photographs. His name was Mr. Peerenboom, an original and evocative sequence of syllables giving us—though you don't have to accept it—a sorely needed new verb.

To peerenboom.

I peerenboom.

Thou peerenboomist.

He peerenbooms.

It's a sorely needed new verb because, as it comes into general usage—'Good evening, Sir Laurence, I've just dropped in to peerenboom you for your brilliant performance tonight'—it will define precisely what one is trying to do, thereby neutralizing the normal British reaction to thanks, which is the immediate suspicion that:

75

(1) the michael is about to be removed

(2) money is on the verge of being borrowed

(3) someone is trying to get in, or out, without paying

(4) a toffee-nosed and patronizing attitude is being adopted which, if it continues much longer, will receive its just reward of a belt up the bracket

(5) not a single word of it is meant, anyway, so kindly don't bother—now or at any future time.

Peerenboomery, or possibly peerenboomination, will cure all that, representing as it does an expression of thanks—for services rendered or pleasure received—of an entirely genuine nature, and therefore to be accepted as such without verbal or physical lashings back.

Some peerenboomatory, for instance, would have been of the greatest help to me the other evening when I was moved— a miracle as astonishing as water gushing from the rock—to try to thank the manager of a vile, shiny, garish, pretentious pull-up for carmen—but that was an attitude that developed only later.

In the beginning I was delighted with the place. It was wide open and bright and gay, an unbelievable jewel in the hopeless waste of a Sunday evening in London. The décor was charming, spacious and gracious with delightful beechwood furnishings. *All* the waitresses were bright and gay and unusually pretty. The food was crisp and fresh and perfectly cooked. Even the coffee was superb. All this was clearly due to the good offices of the manager, a smiling little man in a black coat and striped trousers, who was here, there and everywhere, in and out of the kitchens and round and about, conducting the whole affair with the panache of Sir Malcolm (Flash Harry) Sargent.

I was seized with an uprush of gratitude. I called the bright and gay and pretty waitress. 'May I speak to the manager for a moment, please?'

Her lovely eyes narrowed. The pearly teeth set like a rat-trap. 'What's the matter? You got a complaint?'

'Oh, no, no, no, no, *no!* I merely wish to thank him for running this charming café so charmingly. . . .'

There was a family party at the next table—litter of children, harassed parents and a crone of a grandmother in a brown velour hat based upon the general configuration of a Gladstone bag. She was chumbling cake, but eased off to say to her daughter, through it, 'Squiffed, en 'e?' The daughter prudently moved the nearest child away from me.

'You want to thank the manager?' the waitress said, coming right round to the squiffed theory herself. 'I—I'll see what he says.'

It took her several minutes to catch up with his humming-bird dartings to and fro, and nearly as long, once she'd nailed him, to convey the burden of my incredible message. A man of resource, he acted swiftly. He shot into the kitchen, and stayed there. I took my thanks out of his vile, shiny and pretentious café, and dissipated them on the hopeless Sunday evening air.

If, however, I had announced them to be peerenboominatious, I have no doubt whatever that they would have been most graciously received.

24

Jam on Her Ladyship's Doo-da

THE moment I banged the front door I had a sense of loss, almost of amputation. I'd been deprived of something, cut off from a vital accessory. It turned out to be the latch-key, lying in full view on the table just inside the window. A large, basement window, steel-framed, locked on the inside.

There was, however, hope, an opening, a channel of approach to the key, in the form of a ventilatory pane hinged outwards at the top.

At a time like this the all-round man doesn't panic. He doesn't start breaking windows, shouting for help, ringing the fire brigade or the police. He stands there and thinks. He examines ways and means. He remains steady, the brain, the nerves packed in ice.

I'd reached the idea of a longish pole—a broom handle, possibly—with glue on the end of it, this tacky end to be applied to the key until fusion took place, and then the whole apparatus slowly and carefully lifted out through the ventilatory panel when the dustmen arrived.

At first I thought of leaving them in ignorance of the key situation and of going for a walk round the block, suspecting that broom handles with glue on the end of them might seem a foolish, even a juvenile concept to men as rugged, as physical, as these dustmen, but then I reasoned that their cart, filled as it was with a vast miscellany of debris, might well contain the ingredients of which I stood in need. In fact, taking a positive view, dustmen with a dustcart could easily be looked upon as providential arrivals, in the present impasse.

They didn't have a broom handle, but they did have a long, cardboard tube which might at one time have held a map or a poster. We considered for a time sucking so fiercely at the top end of the tube that the key would fly up it. This plan was rejected, however, on the probable inadequacy of the lungs, coupled with the fear that if they *were* strong enough the key would probably finish up in the stomach of the sucker, leaving us far worse off than before. Steady, competent, all-round men, we turned to a new plan.

From the cart we selected a piece of orange peel and inserted it into the end of the tube, so that it formed a kind of shallow cup. No glue could be found so we filled the cup with raspberry jam from a broken jar. One of the dustmen remembered shooting some honey into the cart earlier in the morning, and offered the opinion that it might be more adhesive than jam. He was, however, unable to find it among the rubbish, so we proceeded with the apparatus in hand.

Everyone was eager, of course, to have first stab with the scientifically jammed tube, and in support of their claim to priority offered suggestions, concerning technique, which only they would be able to execute with the necessary precision. One was in favour of a twisting motion, to embed the key in the jam. Another stood by a single, firm jab. A third maintained that the jam should be held in contact with the key for a minute or so, to give it time to set. While this discussion was in progress something happened which I'd hoped wouldn't. The leading dustman noticed that the key was lying on top of Face Tanner No. 80, or Lady Pamela Berry's aluminized cardboard horse-collar. 'You don't want to get jam on that, mate,' he said—and then, unfortunately—'What is it?' They were all peering through the window, looking at Face Tanner No. 80.

There was no way to hedge or prevaricate, so I gave it to them straight. '. . . wrote a piece in the newspaper about sun-bathing in urban backyards and Lady Pamela Berry does it too, so she was kind enough to send me a Face Tanner. It opens up and fixes round the back of your neck so your face is framed in a kind of aluminium shield. It intensifies the sun's rays. . . .'

They digested it, nodding slowly to themselves. Then the leading dustman had a question which, in the circumstances, seemed unimportant. 'Lady Pamela Berry? Who's she?'

'She's the President of the Incorporated Society of London Fashion Designers,' I said, glad in a way to keep off the more complex subject of the Face Tanner.

They all nodded again. 'Well,' said the leading dustman, 'we wouldn't want to get jam on her ladyship's doo-da so we best shift the key on to the tablecloth. Bit of jam won't do your cloth any harm.'

What we succeeded in doing, with the non-jammed end of the cardboard tube, was to shift the key off Face Tanner No. 80 on to the floor, where it rolled under the table, bringing the salvage operation to an end.

When the owner of the house returned from shopping half an hour later—I'd been sitting on the dustbin in the area, waiting —she said she hoped I hadn't found the interval too boring. I could have replied that much of the time had been fairly well filled with trying to poke the key off Lady Pamela Berry's aluminized horse-collar with a long cardboard tube, one end of which the dustmen had blocked with a piece of orange peel, before filling it with raspberry jam. My actual reply was, 'No, not at all.'

The other, even now, was already beginning to seem untrue.

25

The Handing Over of the Perks

A NUMBER of people had been talking for a long time, on Spanish burgundy, about inflationary wage spirals, falling production, crashing trade returns, tottering stock markets, the increase in rail fares, the rising cost of living, the upsurge of wildcat strikes—saying that they were happening, that is, and that unless the Government did something about it it was their considered opinion that things would get worse.

One cannot sit around for ever, on Spanish burgundy, without some constructive thought entering the mind, even in the field of politics and economics, so shortly after midnight I said I had a solution to the whole thing.

A man called Minch—or Manch—was talking at the time, giving it, with deceptive seriousness, as his view that full unemployment was the only logical solution to Communist-inspired industrial unrest, so I had to lean fairly hard on the voice-box to get the message through.

'The whole trouble is that even in this affluent society a profound dichotomy still exists between worker and employer.' It took. There was a general furrowing of brows, a perceptible apprehension breaking out about cleverness to come—a workmanlike method of gaining attention. I was able to proceed in less weighty vein.

'Despite profit-sharing schemes and other placatory mechanisms about which I know almost nothing the worker still believes the employer is getting an excessive whack of the gravy. This leads to strikes for an extra spoonful, which leads to the price of everything going up, which leads to more strikes, and if this isn't going to go on for ever some concession will have to be made by one side or the other. Now'—Minch was looking restive—'the employers aren't going to cut their profits because they've got their shareholders on the backs of their necks and new plant to buy and a lot of other capitalist obligations, and the workers certainly aren't going to accept lower wages because there's something about getting less for doing the same amount that revolts the very soul. So it's deadlock, and we continue to slide into the abyss.'

'Will this take very long?' Minch said politely.

'Under the hour, without interruption. In this deadlock there is one gesture which could be made which would release the whole thing. In this deadlock there is one adjustable injustice. Who is getting something from the general set-up to which, in terms of strict fair play, he is not entitled? The employer.'

'You don't look like a shop steward,' Minch said. 'But you might be having a night off.'

'I see it,' I went on with some speed, 'as a day of national carnival in some large open space like Salisbury Plain. Bingo, sideshows, roller-coasters, beer tents, qualified nurses in compounds to look after the kiddies—the whole panoply of British fiesta. Then, at midday, comes the ceremony, heralded by the National Anthem played in its entirety by the band of the Coldstream Guards, the ceremony of the Great Renunciation, or the Handing Over of the Perks.'

'Why do you want to hand over the parks?' Minch asked. 'What's the good of that?'

'The Handing Over of the *Perks*. Down the central, flag-bedecked avenue comes a glittering procession of limousines, driven by business executives wearing sackcloth and ashes. Each car bears a placard, varied according to individual guilt complexes, but all based on the theme of the leading vehicles, "Never Paid a Tosser for It—All on the Firm". Then comes a kind of Moral Rearmament, but healthier, public confession, amplified over the whole area—"the villa on the Riviera belongs to the Board and so does the yachtie and the wife's furs and jewellery are represented on the balance sheet as contingencies but from now on I'm going to be a good boy and live in the style to which my wages condemn me, just like all you honest, uncorrupted workers gathered here today——" Good-natured cheers and huzzahs from the crowd, and the purged executives are carried off shoulder high to the jellied-eel tent, where they pay for their own half-pint of wallop in cash——'

It fired their liberal-humanist imaginations. Even Minch said it was just the kind of break-through that the spiritually flaccid Western world had been waiting for. On the way home I tried it on the taxi driver, an elderly man with a somewhat bitter expression. 'What do you, personally, think about all these tycoons who get yachts and cars and haciendas in the West Indies given to them, free, gratis and for nothing by the firm? Do you think it's right?'

The old man paused briefly to shout something a little unforgivable at the female driver of a minicab. He leant back through the window. 'Y'dead right I think it's right. Only wish I had half those geezahs' brains.'

I reflected that someone else was right, too. Minch, on the subject of the spiritually flaccid Western world.

26

Cynthia, Looking Horribly Lovely

I T FELT, and the gathering looked, as though the time might be around 2 a.m.

A going-home restlessness in the air, coupled with a determination to remain to the bitter end—these contrary states of mind evenly divided between some of the husbands and wives, so that voices were beginning in certain quarters to get an edge to them and surprise to be expressed that anyone should want another one after all they'd had already.

A lot of people were sitting on the floor, shouting into one another's face about *Luther* and John Osborne. Three women were sitting together on the sofa, heads together, three pairs of eyes, needle-pointed, dissecting an older woman with sufficient gaiety and vitality left to entertain a number of men standing round the fire.

I detached myself from the *Luther*-Osborne group, goaded beyond endurance by a youth with a goat-like ginger beard who'd just asked me, point-blank, if in fact I had seen the play at all, and if not how did it happen that I had so many clear-cut opinions about faults in its construction. I don't know how he'd spotted this deficiency in my artillery. Also, I didn't like the way in which he was shaping up to run the subject into the ground. 'Tell me,' he said, 'when the curtain rises on Act One how many people—if it doesn't strain your memory too far—are visible on-stage?'

I advised him either to grow a moustache and complete the ludicrous business half begun by the tuft of hair on his chin or, preferably, to shave off the whole ill-conceived project, get his hair cut at the same time and make some perfunctory start

27

Break That Wand, it's Unwanted

THE way I like a trick—card, conjuring, mind-reading, woman-sawing—to be performed is quick, just the bare routine uncluttered by witty patter, magic wands, puffs of smoke or other Merlin razzmatazz, and the moment it's reached its conclusion I want a clear explanation—in the likely event that I've been baffled—of how it was done.

Unexplained tricks are a barbarian assault upon the dignity, upon the very structure, of the civilized mind. We are not now in the Middle Ages, when an illiterate populace required supernatural wonders, miracles and portents to give it something to chumble over in its rude hovels of a winter's evening, before the arrival of mass education, rotary printing, radio and television gave every man the power of rational, independent thought.

No rationally minded man enjoys being mystified nor, if he has any regard for his hard-won intellectual status, should he enjoy mystifying. I propose, therefore, for reasons which will be made apparent at the very earliest opportunity, to reveal in its entirety the whole puerile routine of a trick which totally baffled three international bankers and a distinguished economist one Sunday evening in 1922.

They were attending a soirée at my father's house and, being off-duty and in frivolous mood, their melon-sized brains turned to conundrums, palindromes and mathematical marvels connected with the number nine. It was my mother, the female end of our act, who suggested that we should perform 'the newspaper trick', one in which I'd been able to co-operate with her since the age of five.

I paddled out of the room in my little rompers while she

invited the bankers and the economist to choose any number between nought and twenty. Her nipper would then be summoned to return when she, by spreading a newspaper on the floor and placing coins upon it in various mystic, metaphysical, trigonometrical and Arabic patterns, would be able to convey even to his partially fledged mind the very number upon which their giant intellects had hit.

It worked, as it always did, with foolish ease. She spread out the newspaper, knelt before it in profound contemplation, and then with finicky care, using the right or psychic hand, arranged a shilling, five pennies and a threepenny bit in a trigonometrical pattern all over the page.

The melon-brains watched intently, working out angles, cosines and other relevant data. I had a simpler task. I had only to look at my assistant's left hand, placed unobtrusively on the floor as she leant forward, mystically to arrange the coins with her right. The index finger was sticking out, starkly representing the number one.

She picked up all the coins, and did it again, arranging them this time in an ellipse, with the threepenny bit and two of the pennies pointing at a tangent NNE. Her left hand, placed on the floor, was clenched, indicating no further addition to the original number of one. I was able to give it to the melon-brains shortly afterwards. It was, indeed, their selection. The economist was so shocked he gave expression to a blasphemy.

We did it for them again and again. They drew maps and geometrical designs on the backs of envelopes. They conferred in corners in whispers, getting into bitter argument. When we revealed the basis of our little deception I, at the age of nine, could not remember ever having seen four more explosively angry men.

We should, of course, have told them how it worked after the first successful coup, so that everyone could have a good laugh and get on to something more nourishing. In the same way as this man who's plaguing me from Dublin with his mind-reading act should let me know by return of post how—if it's successful, and, of course, it's bound to be—he did it.

Letters have been pouring in for the last ten days. 'Do exactly as I tell you, no more, no less. Be sure you understand each item of the procedure, before acting, then tick it off, so that you may move straight through the sequence without fault.'

The sequence is one of infantile content. Shuffle the pack, cut, cut again, divide pack into two approximate halves, choose one half, select card from this half, 'make a written memorandum of the identity of this card', put it back in the other half, and mail either half of the pack back to him, without intimating whether it's the half that contains the chosen card. 'You must then,' he says, 'concentrate deeply on the card I have chosen, to assist the transference of human thought over hundreds of miles of sea and land. . . .' The usual Merlin jazz. I am then to 'hold myself in patience for the final phase of the experiment'.

Patience is not the emotion in which I'm holding myself, having posted half the pack three days ago. It's more a sense of pending outrage at injustice. I've revealed how my trick is done. Why can't he do the same? If he doesn't, what is the point of all this miserable, mediaeval mumbo-jumbo?

P.S. He's just done it. It's impossible, but he's got it right. The three of spades. *In re* the explanation of the puerile technique? Mediaeval silence.

Thank you very much, indeed.

28

The Impossible Mrs. Claus

ONE Christmas Eve some years ago I interviewed no less than seven Fathers Christmas at the same time in a pub in Kensington High Street, laying out—as I remember it—three stouts, two light ales, one port and a ginger wine in an effort to stimulate the old gentlemen into sensational revelations about their work.

It was a sticky gathering in every way. Two of the Fathers Christmas were sufficiently hard of hearing to compel me to bawl my questions into their ears—'Do you find that little girls are less demanding than little boys?', etc.—so loudly that the manager came over and asked me, misunderstanding the purpose of the meeting, to leave them pore ole gents alone.

Another Father Christmas, the port drinker, revealed that his Claus work was merely a seasonal and unworthy interruption to his true profession, which was that of providing the voices of rabbits and similar fauna in radio plays for children. 'I wouldn't,' he said, 'give you a tosser for this lark. There's no actin' in it worth speakin' about.' This was clearly a shaft aimed at the oldest Father Christmas, a white-haired, pink-cheeked natural who quavered several times: 'Queen Mary, God bless her, used to come and see me every year. She said I was the nicest Father Christmas what she'd ever seen.'

I left the seven Fathers Christmas in querulous altercation about the merits of the modern method of gift-distribution. The port-drinking, rabbit-talking Claus was in favour of the ticket system, whereby each child received a number at the door and subsequently a parcel corresponding to it, whereas Queen Mary's favourite thought it should be left to Father Christmas

himself. 'A little dollie for the little girls,' he said, 'and a toma-
hawk or a puff-puff for the little boys. That's how I do it and
Queen Mary said I was the nicest Father Christmas what she'd
ever seen. . . .'

The whole *recontre* left me with a strong desire to make no
further enquiries into this aspect of the Christmas myth. A de-
personalized Father Christmas, all white whiskers and jollity,
seemed more in tune with the season of the year than the thought
of a part-time actor counting the weeks until he could get back,
in the face of fierce competition, to providing dramatic dialogue
for Peter Rabbit; and yet news from America has suddenly re-
aroused my interest in the whole Father Christmas *œuvre*.

The news is that in a large San Francisco store Father Christmas
has been lumbered with a wife. A determined-looking matron,
dressed in spangles and a bustle, now stalks the aisles. She is none
other than Mrs. Santa Claus, and by the sound of her advance
publicity she is here to stay.

'This Mrs. Santa Claus thing,' says an official of the store,
'is going to grow and grow. The idea is that Mrs. Santa Claus
gets tired of staying up there in the North Pole. After all, Santa
Claus is gone every Christmas, so she gets fed up. She decides to
come with him. Well, you can imagine all the new avenues this
opens up for us. . . .'

I can imagine one new avenue it might open up for me,
faced in only 364 days' time with the need for yet another piece
of Christmas cheer. An interview with Mrs. Claus herself . . .

I intercept her as she prowls through the Boulevardier's
Boutique, a department devoted to gifts for the man who has
everything. She wears a sweeping, Gay Nineties gown in red
velvet, edged with cotton wool, and a pixie hood to match. She's
a woman of mature years and commanding presence and I'm
sure I've seen her before playing a walk-on duchess—part of a
fashionable crowd of nine—cheering home the winner in a
B-picture about doping at Royal Ascot.

'Excuse me, Mrs. Claus, may I ask you a question?'

'Socks, tays, henkerchiefs to the rait—stret throo for sweed jeckets, dressing gohwns, sports weah——'

'No, no, Mrs. Claus. A personal question. How long have you and Mr. Claus been married?'

She abandons the public-address system to subject me to a narrow, personal examination. Her blue-lidded eyes look wary. She suspects a banana-skin. 'All enquairies concerning staff should be referred to the meneger——'

'This is just a private little chat, Mrs. Claus, for world-wide publication, and if the Press Council objects, round about mid-summer, to this intrusion upon personal privacy we can always maintain that you and Mr. Claus are figures of national interest. The fact is, Mrs. Claus, I find it difficult to believe that you and Mr. Claus are man and wife.'

'Well, the ideah!'

'Your alleged husband, Mrs. Claus, is—or was—a saint. St. Nicholas. Unless he's been de-canonized I don't see how you could have dragged him to the altar. Perhaps you'd like to make a statement. I'm your friend.'

Mrs. Claus, who never wanted the job and wouldn't have taken it if she hadn't been a bit long in the tooth for panto, starts yelling for the house detective. The interviewer is subsequently bought off with the offer of a free pair of socks.

The Establishment, the old British decencies, have bitten the dust yet again.

29

Charge it Up, and Charge me Down

A VOICE on the telephone, brisk, confident, quick-fire, fires itself so quickly that the name sounds like Mr. Vaster. Or Mr. Masters. Or is it Faster? Or even Mister. It's inconceivable that he's called Mr. Mister. A. Mister, Esquire. . . .

Speculation about his identity deprives me of almost the whole of Mr. Mister's message, except for the two dread nuggets that he's public relations, and that he's got a little proposition which he would like to discuss over a bite of lunch.

Two courses are open to me; the only courses, indeed, open to a man who is sane, busy and professional. The first is to tell Mr. Mister to stop sparkling and enticing and to announce his name, the nature of his business, and what he wants me to do for him, spelling out any word I think I may have misheard. The second thing I can do is to tell Mr. Mister that I will meet him in his office any morning at ten o'clock, provided that he supplies, at the outset of the meeting, a typewritten statement of who and what he is and—equally important—another typewritten statement of who and what he thinks *I* am. Under either of these conditions our business together can be conducted with clarity and dispatch.

Instead of doing either of these things I tell Mr. Mister I should be delighted to meet him for a bite of lunch and have a chat about his little proposition because it's the system and there's free drink and I might get a cigar. I don't mention the latter considerations because I know that Mr. Mister knows that I'm considering them already.

We meet, in the congested bar of a derisively expensive restaurant. Mr. Mister's fifth, public-relations sense leads him to me instantly, though we have never met before. He sprays out vitality from his carnation, his dark, gleaming suit, the white shirt with the bold black stripes, the knitted silk tie. I go over him carefully—a matter of routine. At current prices for haberdashery, suiting and accessories Mr. Mister represents about 125 guineas, live on the hoof. Currency undoubtedly stands behind Mr. Mister, but unfortunately another gentleman is present for the clear purpose of seeing that most of it remains there.

His name is inaudible—Mr. Mumble?—and his position in Mr. Mister's firm is unspecified, but I know exactly why he's here. He's the memory man, the recorder, the assessor, the analyser, the brain packed in ice who will tell Mr. Mister, when lunch is over, what happened, if anything does.

Mr. Mumble has a medium sherry. Mr. Mister and I, the Bohemians, the unpredictable geniuses, the think-men, slash into large vodkas-and-tonic. Mr. Mister starts to make friends. He congratulates me on the brilliance of a piece which his wife actually cut out but has now lost. As far as I can identify it it was written by Paul Jennings, about four years ago. I tell him it wasn't much, and then I make a move. 'Exactly what is this little proposition of yours all——'

The head waiter is standing beside us with the usual menu, the size of a hoarding, so we roam through that for a while and settle in the end for smoked salmon and fillet steak. On the way into the restaurant Mr. Mister pauses to influence friends at another table. By the time he rejoins us Mr. Mumble and I have finished our smoked salmon. 'Well,' says Mr. Mister, throwing himself down, 'I take it you've put Peter in the picture——'

He's wrong on two counts. The name isn't Peter and Mr. Mumble and I have been talking in a strained way about Algiers. 'Well,' says Mr. Mister, 'let's not talk biz till we've eaten, eh?' Instantly, after a dagger-like glance at the friends at the other table, he starts talking business with Mr. Mumble. It clearly has no connection with our little proposition because Mr. Mister begins, 'If Gatsonides thinks he can get colour for that price he can think again. . . .' Mr. Mumble eventually deflects him back to me.

'Well, now,' I say to Mr. Mister, 'what's this little proposition of yours all abou——' The waiter skates right into the middle of it, wanting to know what the gentlemen will have in the way of liqueurs. The suggestion of Strega leads Mr. Mister off into a long anecdote about two smashing Italian bits who happened to be in the villa at a time when Mr. Mister was absolutely sure that Mrs. Mister was getting rid of his hard-earned lob in the Casino, and when she suddenly appeared. . . .

I ask for Armagnac, and accept a cigar. I'm prepared to wait, probably until closing time, for Mr. Mister to put his proposition and then I'll slowly demolish it, red-faced, dizzy, stuffed, in no shape for work of any kind.

And tomorrow morning the phone will ring and a little proposition and a bite of lunch and the whole thing will go on in a boozy, useless dream.

30

In with an Inner Mongolian

EXTRAORDINARY as Martians, or human cosmonauts emerging from moon-viewing capsules, they manifested themselves on public, licensed premises the other night, speaking English, holding English pints of beer and wearing overcoats in the saloon bar in accordance with the immemorial English rite.

Two under-secretaries, no less, from the Russian Embassy out and about in the free night world of London and readily available, so far as one could judge, for fraternization, interrogation and the exchange of news and views in general.

They were ordinary, youngish, undistinguished-looking men of modest, not too flush demeanour, with nothing to separate them from the native patrons save for a certain complement of gold teeth.

Two Russians on parole from the Kremlin annexe in Kensington Palace Gardens, out and about in the free night world just like anyone else, and being treated as such by the native patrons preoccupied as ever with their own concerns, in this case pay-pauses, go-slows, rail strikes and the clogging of the post, the normal background to the English scene. In fact, no one was talking to them at all, except the landlord, who was good enough to introduce me, fortifying the gesture with the announcement that I worked for a newspaper.

Fearful that this might lead to an immediate severance of diplomatic relations, I told them at once that I was having a night off, that the most trivial exchange of remarks between the three of us would be treated as top secret. The thinner, paler one terminated these reassurances by saying, with a warm and friendly smile: 'Why is that? I tell you all you want to know.'

The variety seemed to be so great. Resident population in the Siberian salt-mines? What really happened to Beria? Is anyone actually gunning at the moment for Father Khrushchev? The names and addresses of a few lesser spies? The questions seemed a little too heavily loaded for the beginning of international friendship. A milder approach. . . .

'Do you feel yourself to be living in the middle of enemy territory, locked away there inside the Russian Embassy?'

He turned to his friend with a smile less warm and friendly, this time, than humorously resigned, then turned back to me with the answer.

'But why should this be? I am the same as you are. We are all brothers, all friends.'

'But if we're all brothers and all friends why did you stick up that wall in the middle of Berlin to keep us apart?'

He smiled again, quite happily. He was enjoying our little chat. 'That is Germany, not Russia. I know only about my own country.'

The other one nodded in agreement. An irrelevant note had been introduced into a previously interesting conversation. They had obviously expected something better than this.

'What about these rumours we hear about secret police, people removed from their beds in the middle of the night for political offences, and never seen again?'

I had to allow that it sounded fairly offensive, but I guessed that these comradely under-secretaries would take it in good part. They did. 'You speak of tyranny?' said the thin one. 'I tell you something. I am Mongolian. . . .'

'You certainly don't look it.'

'Inner Mongolia. People will tell you this is a slave state, under the Soviet heel. . . .'

'The first I've heard of it. . . .'

'But I, a Mongolian, am under-secretary in the Soviet Embassy in London, with my own apartment, my own car, so how can I be a slave?'

The taste began to insinuate itself of what some of the proceedings at the Security Council must have been like. I passed—to a more general question.

'Do you find that life in London looks—feels—very rich after Inner Mongolia?'

Both of them greeted the enquiry with the greatest good-humour. They explained, giving details of various Plans, that everyone in Russia—and that went for Inner Mongolia, too—would be rich, with cars and television sets and their own houses, in twenty years' time. 'Then,' the thin one said, 'everybody will be happy.'

'But a lot of people in this country have cars and television sets already, and they aren't very happy at all.'

'It will be different in Russia,' they said. 'We will show you.' Both of them, beaming, shook me warmly by the hand and slung their hammer and hook.

Thinking about it afterwards, I realized I'd probably become over-excited by the potentialities of free discussion with a couple of Russian diplomats in a London pub. After all, they're just the same as we are—all brothers, all friends.

In fact, we're so exceedingly friendly there seems to be nothing else to talk about except the weather.

31

Roll on Something

THE emotional climate of Monday, February 5th, when we were all waiting for the world—through an unfortunate concatenation of planets—to come to an end, seemed to the more sensitive among us to be nothing out of the ordinary, just another day, in fact, of cowering in a corner with the breath sucked in and one arm defensively raised, waiting for the worst to occur at last.

It's a posture which has become the norm for the more sensitive type of Western Man, one which he's been holding so long that the defensive arm is tiring and beginning to droop.

It's the waiting that's taking the stuffing out of us, the waiting for the final holocaust that never seems to develop, although we get strong whiffs of it from time to time. Like last Monday week, when the Automobiles conquered London, pouring in like locusts, settling chokingly upon the city in a reeking, duotone flood.

Everyone knows that this will be a permanent feature of urban life by 1965, but all that Western Man can do about it is to wait. We've all become waiters, in fact, and are in general agreement that it's the most wearing occupation in the world.

We seem to have been waiting for ever to enter the Common Market, for Colonel Glenn to take off, for General de Gaulle to be blown up, for someone even less agreeable than Khruschev to mount the throne in the Kremlin, and the longer we wait the more burdensome does the waiting become.

The list of things we've been waiting for, hoping that they're not going to happen, seems to stretch before us to the end of time.

99

We've been waiting for a pause in the pay pause in the certain knowledge that it will provoke even more strikes than the pay pause itself. We've been waiting for I.C.I. to gobble up Courtaulds, or vice versa, and are reduced to the exhausted opinion that it's high time one or the other got on with it. We've also been waiting for the completion of that subterranean jig-saw puzzle at Hyde Park Corner, so that we can taste the aroma of a traffic jam underground. Waiting and waiting, day after day, one arm defensively raised—although here and there, of course, the more resolute type of Western Man fills in the time with active preparations to cushion himself against the final blow.

The Americans are inverting their swimming-pools to contrive shelters against the Bomb and spend their week-ends down there practising survival, armed to the teeth against casual visitors.

An Englishman I met the other evening had taken to learning Russian in the belief that the Atomageddon, as he called it, is scheduled for this coming summer. 'When,' he said, 'I'm incarcerated behind radio-active barbed wire in a concentration camp on the Yorkshire moors I want to be able to ask for another helping of turnips in their own language.'

This was condemned as a short-time and frivolous notion by another man who was learning Chinese. 'The Yellow Peril,' he said—and we've been waiting for *that* for quite some time—'is what you really want to keep your eye on. They'll be doing the Russians any minute now and it'll be our turn next.'

Agitation is even breaking out among the Irish people in this country, a race not normally given to long-term planning. We're getting tired of waiting for an authoritative statement about whether there is or is not a £90 million deposit of minerals under that field in Loughrea. 'If,' as a distinguished emigré publican put it to me recently, 'there's ninety million quid lyin' around at home I might havta think twice about stayin' on here.' In his opinion the exodus had begun already. 'Two fellas I heard of,' he said, '*two* fellas up-staked and went back only last week.'

I ventured the opinion that they might not be too welcome. 'If there's only ninety million there and four million resident inhabitants to get the benefit of it they're going to be chary about the rest of us pouring back. There'll be field guns planted at the mouth of the River Liffey and they'll open up on the transport ships bringing home the Sons of the Gael. And if we turned round again and tried to go back to England we might easily find that the English had passed this Immigration Bill of theirs at long last and they wouldn't let us land even in Liverpool, either.'

'We'd be stuck,' agreed the publican sombrely, 'like the Flying Dutchman, backwards and forwards across the Irish Sea for ever. I wish they'd all make up their minds.'

It's the waiting that's taking the stuffing out of us, the waiting for the blow that never quite falls.

Still, there's one consolation. The Budget is rapidly approaching, and that cannot be postponed. It should constitute enough of a blow for anyone.

32

Genghiz Khold and his Catartars

THAT faint, fairy-needle prickling at the back of the nose, the sensation that the body, waking from sleep, is a shade too warm around the chops, the merest hint too chilly on the extremities, arouse in combination the flicker of a suspicion that the Common Cold may have been caught yet again.

Lie still, cold catcher. Fight! It's psychosomatic. It's all in the mind. Your luck, cold catcher, cannot be running this low.

Only five days ago you met a man bunged up, red-eyed, remote, cut off from human kind in his privately steaming, seething world and you said to him, keeping your distance: 'I know—they're terrible. I'd a fearful one only——'

And then the realization that you could not remember the precise moment, the hour, the day, when the scourge had lifted off its burning claws, when hot flushes and icy chills had blended into the normal sub-normal temperature, when the chest-cracking tinder-dry cough had been mollified by—what?—over-use, coughing parts wearing out . . . ?

At all events, it had gone, and a period had intervened when no cold was in progress, a sensation probably similar to being given compassionate week-end leave from jail—i.e. joy in the present, overshadowed by the certainty that you'll be for it again very shortly.

And here it is—a really splendid one, a champion right up there in the heavyweight division. That fairy-needle prickling never lies. Soon, now, the invading hordes of microbes—I once heard them described as Genghis Khold and his Catartar raiders —will possess the whole head and chest, bunging up ears, eyes, nose and lungs, reducing the very soul to a wet handkerchief.

How, you wish to know, does the experienced cold catcher react to catching yet another cold, having had three beauties already since Christmas? What preventive or therapeutic measures does he take, in view of the fact that if this sort of thing goes on he must surely be heading for an early grave?

The experienced cold catcher does nothing at all! No pill, no tablet, no cough-drop passes his burning lips. Nothing is spread on, sniffed up or gargled. Masterly inaction is the experienced cold catcher's portion, for the solid and sufficient reason that no pill, no tablet, cough-drop or other medicament has ever been known to do him the slightest good. This negative action not only saves money but also hours of time that might otherwise be squandered upon pill swallowing, gargle mixing, kettle boiling, linctus swilling, to say nothing of the endless journeys backwards and forwards to the chemist, and certainly not to mention the greatest waste of all—i.e. the time spent in waiting for these medicaments to make one feel a little better, before one's time.

There's a futile exercise, beneath the experienced catcher's contempt. He knows what happens when Genghis Khold and his Catartar raiders breach the fortifications. No power on earth can get them out until they've done their usual thorough job of looting, sacking and burning, and least of all a mere gargle or a tablespoonful of lung tonic. Once the raiders get in they stay, until they're good and ready to pack up and go and assault someone else, leaving of course a hacking cough behind as a reminder that they'll almost certainly be back in full force round about the week after next.

But, you say—aghast at this evidence of suffering so stoically endured—can't you do something to stop it before it starts? Vitamin pills, injections, yeast, a woolly vest . . . ?

An amusing suggestion, and one which is fairly frequently made by the cold catchers' regular companions, who tend to pick up a certain back-wash from his ill luck.

All kinds of lunatic suggestions are made, of course, in this field. I was speaking to a man only the other evening—I could scarcely see him through the fumes of the cold I'm wearing at the moment—and he told me he had an infallible preventative. The moment, he said, he felt a cold coming on he gave up eating, drank nothing but fruit juice, and lo and behold—his own words—within twenty-four hours the cold had gone. He consumed three large whiskeys while we chatted and he had a real streamer which, he allowed, had taken him unawares, breaching his fortifications before the fruit juice régime had time to set in.

Any experienced catcher could have told him that by the time any identifiable symptoms establish themselves you've already had a cold for two days, and now it wants to get out and about and enjoy itself.

Injections, vitamin pills, yeast? All very well in their way but the temptation to cease the treatment, to see if it's really protecting you from colds, is too great. You knock off, from curiosity, and instantly collect a haymaker.

That, as a matter of fact, is the way I caught the one I'm wearing now.

33

Shoot me the News, Connection

Y OU get an idea of what drug addiction must be like when the boy who delivers the newspapers starts playing crazy with the fix.

Up till a couple of weeks ago my connection was solid—a neat, serious operator of about eleven, with a little duffel-coat, a shiny blue bicycle and a good strong delivery, right through the letter-box on the dot of 7.20 every morning, followed by swift departure before either of us could become involved in greetings or thanks possibly abrasive to the spirit at this early hour.

The system worked beautifully. The rattle of the letter-box gets the client out of bed. First newspaper and first shot during electric shaving process, second newspaper and second shot during egg or smoked haddock boiling, third newspaper and last shot during eating and subsequent period of meditation. The mind filled and soothed with the events of yesterday, and all off smoothly to work.

Then we miss a beat. No newspapers at 7.20! No rattle of the letter-box, no heavy splash as the nutriment hits the hall floor.

The client suffers the faintest frisson of the nerves. Supposing that industrious little lad doesn't come with the fix? There's going to be a gap. There's going to be a hunger. What former well-known actress has died during the night? Is there a man in space? How is the Vicar? Is Hayley Mills going to play Cleopatra? Where *is* that lad? What's he doing?

The letter-box rattles and the nutriment hits the parquet while I'm ringing the newsagent, so that all is well. Three newspapers, three deeply satisfying shots. Lady Olivier and Mr. John Merivale are still dining *à deux*, the Fraud Squad is asking polite questions around Threadneedle Street, the Earl of Snowdon has had a day off from the office. The frisson evaporates. The client is whole again.

Next morning it's the jigs. The fix has not arrived and it's already 7.45! I've got them, all right. Running between the front and back doors, peering from the kitchen window, down the drive in pyjamas in the rain, and the newsagent's telephone is constantly engaged.

I am not prepared to accept the fact that the lad may be ill. Yesterday's delay in the fix has got me jumpy. Neuroses and suspicions are building up. I know that the lad is hale and hearty, and I also know that he's not going to come. For whatever fiendish reason he has, he's not going to come. He's out there, somewhere in the village, strolling about with my fix in his little canvas satchel, and for some mindlessly cruel reason he's going to give my fix to someone else.

There may *be* a man in space. Jack Kennedy may have done something fearful. Shirley Bassey has quite possibly been shot at again. Why am I not allowed to know? Of all the people in the world why should I be deprived of my——

At 8.30 the newspapers are inserted with unspeakable slyness into the letter-box. I snatch open the door. The connection, the neat, serious lad of about eleven, stands outside. It's still raining. His face is framed by the hood of his little duffel-coat. It gives him a strange, ecclesiastical appearance, as though he were some sort of dwarf novitiate monk from an unimaginable order in the Himalayas.

'What's gone wrong? What's happened?'

He must be a Zen Buddhist. My questions mean nothing to him. No flicker of expression crosses his face.

'Why are you late? What's gone wrong?'

'Nothing,' he says, microscopically surprised, and walks away. 'Where's your bicycle?' I shout after him. No reply.

The newsagent is baffled, too. He allows the lad is a bit moody, but boys are hard to get, so there we are.

There we, indeed, are, crouched behind the front door from 7.15 onwards every morning, plucking at the pyjamas, leaping at the slightest sound from outside, crying for it, the mind clawing for the fix. And now he's really got me on the run. He senses where I am in the house. When I'm crouched, shaking, in the hall he leaves them quietly outside the back door. Once, he put his little satchel on the gate, very early, and walked away. I scrabbled through it and found everyone else's papers except mine. He delivered mine at 8.42.

Mostly, now, I read the morning papers at night, when I get home, but the kick has gone. They don't bite, grip, take hold like the morning shot. Everything seems pallid, lacklustre, dehydrated. Perhaps you always feel like that when you're taking the cold turkey, total withdrawal cure. Perhaps it's all to the good. I must have been pretty bad. . . .

Well, do you think that your newspaper boy is a dwarf, Zen Buddhist novitiate monk from a lost order in the Himalayas?

34

No Stringent Shoes

THE reprinting of a mature—in the sense of age rather than quality—piece of mine in an American male fashion magazine called *Gentlemen's Quarterly* brings about, through the study of a free copy on a sombre afternoon, sombre analysis of the whole psyche, with special reference to the bedraggled coverings now hanging in the cupboard.

The gentlemen of *Gentlemen's Quarterly*—or, rather, the male models playing the roles—all appear to be thrusting, imaginative, hard-working, hard-playing executives in the middle thirties, accustomed to Martinis in penthouses and vacations involving yachts in Bermuda. Despite the scope and busyness of their lives, however, they are prepared to expend an extraordinary amount of time—and emotion—on how they look.

They are, for instance, agog over the dramatic spring softening of the Continental and Ivy Styles into the new-new London Line—slightly wider lapel, restrained padding at the shoulder, subdued hip-flaring but definite suppression at the waist. They greet with cheers the arrival of stunningly new, electric-blue blazers in nubby Indian silk. Excitement is equally steamy over the fact that shoes, this season, will be sleekly trim but far from stringent, that sports jackets will have bellows pockets with bi-swing gussets and that giant over-plaids in muted hues will be going places, wherever the smart people meet.

The first, instinctively hostile, reaction to all this is that anyone who has the money is fully entitled to fit himself out with whatever up-to-the-minute haberdashery may catch his fancy, and the best of luck to the flashy little macaroni. Then, the reaction seems too instinctive. The corrective must be applied of sober thought. Like how does it happen that I, on the verge of my forty-eighth birthday, having earned a fair stack of chips in my time, have in my wardrobe no single garment in which a gentleman from *Gentlemen's Quarterly* would wish to be found dead?

The selection of potential shrouds is admittedly limited, but their really depressing feature is that all but one of them have been subjected to a process of erosion as inevitable, seemingly, as the abrasive action of wind and water upon Beachy Head. Four jackets hang in the cupboard, but they lost their trousers years ago. Slowly, imperceptibly, through continuous wear, the seats became transparent, the lighter tears the fob pocket, pipe embers pit the thighs. Then, in a moment of carelessness or hurry, and seeing that they're nearly done anyway, they are used for gardening or golf, it pours with rain and suddenly, yet again, there is for all social purposes only the jacket left. The jackets hang in the cupboard, waiting to ring the changes—and small the change is too—on the pair of ready-made slacks purchased in the interests of decency. Beside them hangs the only complete suit—complete because it's only a year old—but at any moment an unexpected rush of car-cleaning or sink-unstopping will make it scarcely worth while to have the trousers refurbished, and the wardrobe will again contain no complete ensemble for formal wear.

The whole way of life must be rotten. The very soul must be pinched with slovenliness, miserliness and improvidence. Why, in the name of reason, not give a tailor a banker's order of £5 a month for life and order seven suits all at the same time, so that none need be worn more than once a week?

A reasonable plan, and one which meets with an instinctively hostile reaction. How can seven suits be ordered at a time, when it's possible to have seven changes of mind over ordering one? Decide upon the flannel, get home, look at the jackets of two previous flannels hanging in the cupboard, ring the tailor, cancel the flannel, fail to get back for two weeks, chose the muted over-plaid, cancel that. . . .

No one can choose seven suits all at the same time. One

pin-stripe, one chalk-stripe, one check and one worsted. One black, one white and one khaki. In a frenzy of selection, trying to make them all different, you'd finish up with three almost exactly the same, and four unwearable fantasies.

Three almost exactly the same? Why not have *all seven* exactly the same? Taking care, of course, to have them numbered in pairs, so that the right trousers always go with the right jacket, because otherwise, to save the labour of changing over loose currency and wallet, one would go on wearing the same pair of trousers until they fell to pieces, and then start on the next pair until one finishes up with seven jackets all exactly the same and not a single pair of trousers to . . .

Slovenliness, improvidence, miserliness and incompetence.

One would scarcely have guessed that such bitter self-realization would come from the casual reading of a paragraph about shoes, this season, not being stringent, but stunningly, sleekly trim.

35

The Passport Photo Sleeps

ARRIVAL outside the American Embassy in Grosvenor Square at 8.30 in the morning, to claim a parking meter before the full tide of Impalas, Corsairs, Ramblers, Galaxies rolls in. A visa is required, to visit the land of the free.

At this early hour, while the Foreign Office is still probably spreading chunky marmalade on its breakfast toast, the representatives of the New World are rushing eupeptically to work. Lithe third secretaries in narrow-brimmed hats run up the Embassy steps. Stenographers spring out of taxis. A religious service, every seat occupied, is in progress in a kind of basement chapel. At any moment, one feels, it will be time for the American mid-morning coffee break, while the British are still occupied with early-morning tea. The Americans, indeed, have probably gained such a long lead already that the whole Embassy staff will be back home in bed, with a full day's diplomacy behind them, before Lord Home has even had a chance to open *The Times*.

At 8.40 there are already eleven customers, tuned to this dawn drive, waiting outside the visa office. On the dot of nine o'clock the shining glass doors are thrown open and we're welcomed in by positively beaming officials. They deal with our enquiries at such a pace that there is scarcely time to help oneself to the racks of free magazines.

The problems of an American visa have clearly become simplified out of all recognition. No longer is the visitor asked if he intends to shoot the President. There are no enquiries about his emotional leanings in the Spanish Civil War. All that's required, if he's going on business, is a letter stating the purpose of his visit, and one photograph. . . .

And one photograph. With a crunch the whole beaming, smiling, eupeptic, smoothly flowing operation stops. It stops dead, totally broken down.

One photograph, of passport size. A small, blurred representation of the face, a thing that has been created by the miracle of modern science countless times, with expressions grave, gay, thoughtful, soppy, maniacal, even sweet. But have we got one now? Have we, ready to hand, a small square of pasteboard presenting our likeness, without which the smoothly flowing visa machinery cannot work? We certainly, positively and definitely have not. I would like to go further. If, the last time we had a passport photograph taken, we had ordered two thousand prints to be made and had filed the whole lot of them away in a safe in an envelope clearly printed with the label, 'PASSPORT PHOTOGRAPHS', would a single one now remain, available to our hand? I cause myself to laugh, a short, bitter bark.

Not that there is anything, even shortly and bitterly, to laugh at because precisely and soberly speaking, in our present passport-photographless state, we stand upon the edge of the abyss. There is, in fact, no quicker method of plunging yourself into black, howling chaos than by trying to have a passport photograph taken.

Like steak-and-kidney, egg-and-bacon, passport-photographs-and-Oxford-Street walk for ever hand in hand, welded indissolubly together. There is no other street in London in which it's possible to have a passport photograph taken, and that is a fact. It's also a fact that passport photography studios in Oxford Street never occupy the same premises for more than two weeks at a time. In April there's one just near Bond Street Tube station. When you rush back to it in May, in a frenzied hurry, it's turned into a boutique selling foundation garments, and no one within a range of seven miles knows where it's gone to now.

Unspeakable things happen even outside passport photography studios, apart from the feeling of having to hold on to the window to stop the whole place slipping away, or turning into something else.

The Passport Photo Sleeps

At 9.25 the other morning I was bent double, peering under a kind of roller-blind door pulled halfway down, looking at the motionless legs of a passport photographer standing inside, his feet pointing away from me, when I was joined by another man in the worst possible shape for having a passport photograph taken of anyone I'd ever seen. Three days' growth of beard, no tie and intoxicated at 9.25 a.m. We both shouted at the legs asking if they were open yet, but there was no movement or reply. A ludicrous, brain-rocking situation, but nothing out of the way in passport photography.

Neither was the result. The legs turned out to belong to a Maltese. He took my picture. I shot back to collect two hours later. He showed me a thing that looked like Dorian Gray after the blow had fallen. 'She sleeps,' he said. It seemed to have nothing to do with me, until I found out it was my face and the camera had slipped, and we had to do it all over again.

The final result looked like Dorian Gray's father.

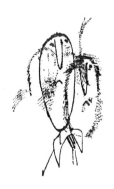

36

America While You Wait

THERE is nothing—and I hope that this somewhat formal opening statement will not cause the intellectual element in the audience to make a break for the exit—like travel to broaden the mind.

Two weeks ago, for instance, before my week-end in America, I would have dismissed as power-crazed drivel the pronouncement made recently in London by Mrs. Evelyn Sharp, American hotels chief, that Britons are hesitant about visiting the U.S.A. because they're frightened of Americans.

I had met many Americans here, like Lena Horne, Gene Tunney, Gipsy Rose Lee and the 'Cisco Kid, and found them the reverse of intimidating—well up to European standards, in fact, in the way of *Gemütlichkeit*, though why our good but somewhat rumbustious friends the Germans should have the nominal monopoly of that virtue is not too easy to tell.

After a week-end in America, however, surrounded by millions of Americans on their home ground, I am forced to the conclusion that to the British visitor the Americans can be very frightening indeed.

No hint of adverse criticism is intended, of course. Absolutely no breath of complaint is being breathed. With Khruschev and Madame Furtseva becoming ever more treacherously cosy, humorous and cuddly this is no time to create schisms on our side of the Curtain, but none the less the personal opinion has to be aired that the home-based American mind works at one-tenth the speed of the European. This, of course, is exactly as it should be. One would be rigidly opposed to precipitate or slapdash ratiocination on the part of the leaders of the Western Alliance, but on the other hand this thoroughness, thought-wise, makes it alarmingly difficult to communicate with our very best friends.

The telephone rings in my hotel room. A representative from City Hall waits below in the lobby to show me round the produce distribution centre, the foundations of the new police head-quarters, three railway stations, the mayoral committee room, the main drains and any other facet of municipal life in which I may have a special interest.

In the hope that we may shelve this programme in favour of the bars in the better hotels, a really good sea-food restaurant, all the nightclubs and a safely conducted tour of Skid Row, I infuse gaiety, camaraderie, into the voice. 'Hi, there! Glad to hear from you. I'll be right down. You'll easily recognize me. I'm nearly eight feet high and look like a melancholy ferret. . . .'

There is absolute silence the other end. I fear we have been cut off. There isn't even the sound of breathing. Then I realize that American thinking has been going on. The voice returns, very wary, very polite, diplomatic in the extreme. 'I'm sorry. I guess I'm not right with what you just said. We got a pretty tight schedule so we don't want to get our wires crossed. I'd certainly be obliged if you could repeat your identification.'

'Rather tall.'

'Check.' He gives me his own description, at dictation speed, and I should be writing it down. 'Average stature, mature years, one hundred seventy pounds, bifocals, tan-silk suit.' I thank him. 'You want,' he asks, 'I should give you that again, for verification?'

All the men in the lobby look mature and of average stature and a lot of them are wearing tan-silk suits. My man turns out to be wearing more of a dark-umber suit, and I tell him so in passing —except that we stop right there. The tight schedule is forgotten while we examine the suit under varied lighting conditions. Slowly and carefully he gives me its history—purchased in Baltimore, in 1959, retailing at 175 dollars, only been worn on three previous occasions, always known to his wife as 'the tan-silk suit'. The machinery begins to pick up again, gathering speed. His wife is right outside in the car. We can check with her. Maybe we can reorientate our thinking about the colour of the suit so we can hit a smoother run next time, identification-wise. We do so, in the most scrupulously conscientious detail, until my mind feels as if it's hanging out of my ears. Then we go and look at the main drains.

Fear of Americans has set in so severely that I'm deprived of the power of speech, where speech is taken to include, European-wise, the exercise of mild irony, modest hyperbole or other departure from simple enquiry or plain statement of basic fact.

Not—and it cannot be too heavily emphasized—that one is making a complaint. Rather is it an occasion for rejoicing that the leading defenders of the Western faith should be men of such uniquely ponderous—in the best possible sense of weighty—turn of mind.

It's the kind of steadying influence we need over those wise-cracking, frivolous playboys, Konny Adenauer, Harry Macmillan and Charlie de Gaulle.

37

Watch Out—it's the Murphia!

MANY thinking persons are coming to the conclusion that the segregation of the Irish in Great Britain is now overdue, before their grip on the body social becomes so powerful that it can be loosened only by force.

Externally, of course, it would appear that everything is well. Gratitude might even be felt towards the inexhaustible horde of Irish men and women who, generously prepared to forget seven hundred years of tyrannical occupation, now build all the roads, drainage schemes, factories and flats, serve all the drinks in all the pubs and provide a complete nursing staff for every hospital in the land of their former oppressors.

All this only looks good on the surface. Underneath, the Irish Mafia is working away, relentlessly seeing their own fellas right, at the expense of the native English.

For instance, my natural sense of justice is outraged every time I arrive at a car-park in the very heart of the British Empire, only a step or two from Piccadilly Circus itself. The entrance is always barred by a notice that says, 'FULL UP'. More often than not a captain of British industry, upon whom several thousand Irishmen are dependent for a living, is trying to get his Rolls or Bentley in, to hurry off to a meeting the result of which will be to provide jobs for several thousand more Irishmen, and the Irishman in charge of the car-park will not let him in. I allow the Rolls or Bentley to withdraw, and present myself. The secret language of the Mafia gets to work. 'Hey, you, willya shift that shuddherin' notice before I havta get out an' do it meself. . . .'

The reply is automatic. 'Go on owa that, you. I'm not goin' to rupture meself shovin' that yoke about.' An Englishman would regard this as final, but not a Mafia member. 'Begob, you wouldn't do a hand's turn for your own mother.' 'Be janey, I know who she is, annyway. . . .' After several other official exchanges of this kind, he removes the notice. 'Ah, come on in owa that—you're only gettin' in your own way.' One of our own fellas has been seen right again.

This, however, is a straightforward deal. Both of us know in advance that we are members. The exchange of passwords is necessary only to add a little colour to the day. It's when we're not sure if we're in the presence of a fellow member that the real subtleties break out, and this can occur with increasing frequency, now that the war has been over for sixteen years. The counter-oppression of Britain started, of course, in 1945, when it became safe, and in these sixteen years many members of the Mafia have achieved a protective camouflage impenetrable save by the keenest eye and ear.

The other night I found myself outside a club at the same time as, but not attached to, four British aristocrats who, like myself, wanted to get in. The silvery-haired, impeccably dinner-jacketed manager was exceedingly sorry, but he couldn't facilitate us. The licensing regulations made it impossible for him to accept, without the statutory interval of forty-eight hours, new members. The aristocrats bawled at him for a while, and went away.

There was something about the faintly bat-like set of the ears, the innocent-knowing look in the eye, the steely softness, the whole aura of duality that suggested, despite the impeccable dinner-jacket and the Mayfair-Cockney accent, that he might be a Mullingar man himself, come a long way from behind Morrissey's Select Lounge and Bar.

A tentative showing of the outer edge of the Mafia membership card. Nothing too much, in case an error had been made. Just a slight softening of the vowel sounds. 'Are yah out long?'

It took. He scarcely showed it, but the vital contact had been made. He looked circumspectly up and down the street. 'Give us a quid an' you're in.'

Unfortunately, the system also has a tendency to work in reverse. I was chatting the other evening in another club with a group of English lords and their ladies, touching—perhaps over-imaginatively—upon my close ties with the polo and hunting set in Kildare, inspired by the fact that many of them were well known to my new friends, only to be interrupted by a voice that said, 'God forgive yah, yah big bowsie—th'only t'ing you ever rode in your life was a bike.' I hadn't seen him for fifteen years, but from the way he carried on, for the next hour, one would have thought—and the English lords and their ladies did—that he was my best friend.

There's no doubt that the Irish, in England, are becoming rather too thick on the ground. Segregation would seem to be the only answer, except, of course, for car-park attendants, night-club managers, head waiters and those of us who are able to conceal the fact that we are, as it were, coloured, until—if yah folla me—there's a chanst of it doin' us a bitta good.

38

General Shirtiness, Drip-dried

IT OCCURRED to me the other evening, towards the end of a dinner unclouded up till then by metaphysical speculation, that the fundamental cause of global strife was not, primarily, the machinations of power-crazed politicians but rather the slow expansion of a universal shirtiness, the rising of a general irascibility, from which an outbreak of violence presents the only logical, emotional release. 'Or don't,' I added, to give everyone a chance, 'you think?'

There was a longish silence, and then the hostess said, 'Let's go upstairs, girls, shall we, before all this starts?'

It felt like a duty—even a mission—to make my point clearer, not that it didn't seem to have a pellucid transparency already.

'Everyone,' I said, 'these days is instantly prepared, talking clean off the top of their own prejudices, to ascribe the worst possible motives to everyone else. The unfortunate Hammarskjold is scarcely dead before he's described as a watery-eyed, would-be dictator with a private army of twenty thousand men, ruthlessly intent upon learning the craft of world domination at the expense of the ignorant natives of the Congo. Large numbers of persons who up till then had pictured him—if they even knew what his job involved—as a dull but immensely competent and industrious Swede with an almost inhuman dedication to the task of bringing about peace by negotiation, feel, at the thought of a watery-eyed, world dictator, the adrenalin start pumping, blood pressure going up, teeth grinding, fists clenching, hackles rising—general shirtiness boiling into the air again.'

'How,' someone said carefully, 'can you have a *logical* emotional release? Logic and emotion are surely incompatible?'

I couldn't wait. 'Ah, have another bit of cheese, you. To continue—everyone's griping and binding about everyone else. President Kennedy's only a flash in the pan. Super Mac's gone down the pipe altogether. Selwyn Lloyd's going to bankrupt the whole country. Gaitskell's turned into a Tory reactionary. The trades unions are riddled with conspiracy and corruption. Vanessa, Shelagh, Osborne, Wesker—yah, go and get yourselves a bath, yah beardie-weirdies. Poor old Bertie Russell's soft in the head. What's Sir Dandy (Never Short of a Clean Shirt) Eccles going to do about the starving teachers? Why doesn't that slippery clown Khruschev stop being so cheerful? Yah! Git 'aht of it! Shuddup! You're a liar! You're wrong! Lie down! Drop dead! It's the general shirtiness in the air that does it. It's like a man with a boil on the back of his neck, and gout, hobbling along to Carey Street for his final examination and his wife failed to post his winning pools coupon and the rain is belting down and he trips over a dog and at that moment a small boy with a face like a plate of frogspawn shouts at him, "Git yer 'air cut!", and the man tries to cut off the lad's head with his umbrella. It's the only logical emotional release to the man's general shirtiness, created by a mass of abrasives. It's the thing that really starts wars. . . .'

Instantly, of course, a roar of voices. 'What absolute drivel . . . what do you *mean* by shirtiness . . . do you attempt to deny me the right to openly expressed and reasoned criticism of those Pentagon gangsters . . . of that cynical Kremlin tyrant . . . *prove* that Mr. Harold Macmillan has gone down the pipe . . .'

The following morning rather busy with telephone calls, general apologies, didn't quite mean, bunch of flowers for the hostess, promise to replace certain items of glassware, but it was also illuminated by the discovery that someone else in the country was alive to the dangers of shirtiness, individual and international. Maharishi Mahesh Yogi, a saintly man from India, giving out from his hotel room the very message with which I'd been occupied the previous evening.

The Maharishi, I noted, believed that whatever a man says or thinks creates vibrations of tension in the atmosphere, and *the sum of these tense vibrations explodes into calamities like war.* General shirtiness, in fact, expressed with the grace becoming to a saintly man.

Furthermore, the saintly man had a cure. Everyone must have their own Word, a Word especially attuned to their psyche, and repeat it endlessly to themselves until all shirtiness is murmured away, and only peaceful and beneficial vibrations are allowed to escape into the previously troubled air. The immediate difficulty was that the Word had to be an Indian one.

Impatient, as ever, to bring about world peace, I ranged rapidly through my Tamil and Hindustani dialects, and came up with the following peaceful vibration creators:

Poppadum. Chapatti. Brynjal curry.

Not only did they seem prosaic, even a little greasy, for their elevated purpose, but I couldn't be sure of the spelling, of the possibly catastrophic effect of endlessly murmuring Poppadum when it ought to be Poppa*dom.*

A burst of righteous indignation against saintly Indians who come over here with woolly headed, mystic cures for the hard, practical problems of the Western world brought constructive thought about the whole matter to a not unwelcome end.

39

The Cannibal Establishment

THOSE bright, youngish men from *Beyond the Fringe* are about—if it's possible to believe anything one reads in the papers—to open a new kind of club in Soho, forthrightly to be called The Establishment.

At The Establishment, according to one of the youngish men, there will be late-night revues 'the character of which will depend upon the day-to-day lunacies of our leaders, political and spiritual'.

There's a whistle of fresh air. For too long now West End revues have concentrated upon Noël Coward, débutantes, the Wolfenden Report, and similar frivolities, as subjects for biting satire, so that all thinking persons should be delighted at the new menu promised by The Establishment—the nightly roasting of the Prime Minister, the President of the Board of Trade, the First Lord of the Admiralty, the Archbishop of Canterbury, the Prebendary of the Church of Scotland, the Chief Scout . . .

The list of leaders political, spiritual, etc., suddenly seems to be so long that it creates a sense of top-heaviness, of unbalance, even vertigo. And there is still to come the Lord Chief Justice, the Home Secretary, Black Rod, the Lord Privy Seal, the Red Dean . . . With so many leaders on the job the wonder is that there's anyone left to be led. Thousands of Ministers, Presidents, Chairmen, Bishops, Generals and Judges and all of them, according to these youngish men *Beyond the Fringe*, subject to daily attacks of lunacy, demonstrated in thought, word and deed.

A harsh judgement? One liable to have an adverse effect upon, say, the deliberations of the Cabinet?

The Cabinet is in session round the mahogany in No. 10.

They are reading transcripts of the songs and sketches from The Establishment's revue of the night before, hot from the typist pool in the Lord Chamberlain's office, after under-cover tape-recording by security officers wearing false jeans and beards.

The Lord Chamberlain ought to be in attendance in the ante-room but, in fact, he's at home, in bed. The double duty of keeping an eye on *Fings Ain't What They Used T'Be* and this late-night revue business means he can get to sleep only during the day.

The Cabinet continues to read these scurrilous accusations of lunacy, idiocy, imbecility and cretinism, yet they're not actually reading. They're more leafing through. They're not, by cracky, even doing that! They're simply counting the number of times their names are mentioned and making a note on their blotters and then turning to sneer at Ag. and Fish, who hasn't been pilloried at all.

The P.M., as usual, has come out on top. He stars in five of the sketches and brings down the house at the finale accoutred as a baby, playing with his toes, and lisping, 'This little pig went to the Common Market, and this little pig stayed at home . . .' He has, however, a word of criticism. 'These chaps are slacking,' he observes. 'There was a splendid chance there to have a really woundy dig at the F.O. That last line should read—"and this little pig stayed with Home".' He turns to Dr. Charles Hill. 'You're supposed to be co-ordinating Government public relations, aren't you? Well, co-ordinate.'

Flapped, as usual, only momentarily, his good humour returns. 'As a matter of fact,' he tells the assembled Cabinet, 'I ran up a little something in the bath this morning which I venture to think has a certain merit, and might be worth passing on. It begins, "I wandered lonely as Macleod . . ." '

A great shout of laughter goes up. Ag. and Fish, trying to get back into the act, claps Colonies on the shoulder. 'You're in, boy!' he cries. 'Top of the bill tonight!'

Colonies is deeply gratified. 'Thanks a lot, P.M. Apropos

of your brilliant pig theme I was wondering if there was any-thing in "Old Macmillan had a farm . . ."'?'

The P.M. nods graciously. 'We are already at work upon it. We want to keep the material coming, you know. We've got to keep the Tory image in the forefront of the public mind. I mean, if we can't be more lunatic than Hughie we may as well shut up the shop.'

The foregoing dry run at biting political satire has unfortunately served to convince me that the real victims of The Establishment's new late-night revues are going to be the three bitingly satirical writers themselves. Biting political satire seems to have the opposite effect in this country to the one intended.

The Umbrella Man, derided for his gamp, is now remembered with sentimental affection. The widely publicized lips that Stanley Baldwin sealed around his pipe in time to give the *Luftwaffe* a head start have turned him into as solid a national father-figure as John Bull.

These boys beyond the fringe had better look out. They're stepping into line for O.B.E.s for political services loyally rendered to The Establishment itself.

P.S. The Establishment is now open. None of the young gentlemen are in any danger whatever.

40

Nijinsky of the Lawns

THE call of the lawn-mower is heard through the land as the evenings draw out, the primulas blaze, the lime-green buds start from the dark sticks of the trees and—the greatest stimulus of all—the man next door has made a yellow mess of his bit of grass because anyone can see with half an eye that his mower is on the light side for churning through the *salade Nicoise* that is his reward for inadequate spiking, rolling, feeding, weeding, raking and scratching last year.

But waiting in the shed for the provident husbandman is the massive, reconditioned four-stroke, the very name of which is synonymous with the gleam of the grass in Oxford colleges, with the velvety sheen of the Duke's croquet lawn beyond the lych-gate leading from the rose arbour. Still attached to its handlebars by a piece of thick, white, whiskery string is the strong, sandy-coloured label, guaranteeing by its very coarseness of texture that an English craftsman's job has been done on the regrinding and resetting of the blades, the dismantling and readjustment of the carburettor, decarbonization, the tightening of the driving chains, the changing of the oil, the cleaning and resetting of the sparking plug. They've even given the grass-box a wipe-over with a paraffin rag, so that the royal imprimatur shines out in red and gold.

It's not going to be easy—that one recognizes. The grass is long and lush and wet. But what we do is to set the blades an inch above the ground so that we get, in transatlantic parlance, a crew-cut—an admittedly callow but necessary preliminary to the later, Trumper-clean, dukely, ancient shave. (There's something about the royal imprimatur on that lawn-mower that makes one think of lovely women with foamy parasols, the long shadows of the cedars, officers in pillbox caps who are gentlemen and old gardeners in baize aprons, born in Stoke d'Abernon, with loops of raffia hanging over their ears.)

The goddam' thing won't start. A full tank of petrol, half-choke, half-throttle, a firm but not frantic kick on the starter, and nothing happens at all, except that petrol begins to pour in an urgent stream from the bottom of the newly reconditioned carburettor. Resetting of the choke and the throttle, frantic kicking, firm kicking, a soft, voluptuous stroking of the starting lever result in nothing at all, save for an increasing fear of fire.

Everything that anyone has said within recent years about the British craftsman is true. The Welfare State has diluted his craftsmanship to Danish-type, Benelux-pasteurized skimmed milk with a plastic base. No pride in his work, no joy. Feather-bedding, restrictive practices, irresponsible wage claims, over-time for the tea-break, double overtime for wild-cat strike meetings, production sinking alarmingly, West Germany going ahead, the Commonwealth breaking up, petrol dripping in a steady stream from the bottom of a British reconditioned carburettor. . . .

The assistant in the hardware shop which reconditioned the mower answers the telephone. On a Saturday morning, at the peak time of rural trading, he appears to be the only official there. He can't say himself. He doesn't know. He will try to get someone to come round.

Prepared, by a reflex action, for a three-week interval, I dismantle the carburettor myself. As soon as I loosen the small screws holding down the lid and feel the upward pressure of an unseen spring I know that all is not well, in the same way as I did when I took the back plate off a faulty door-latch and springs, levers, ratchets, washers burst out like the components of a Roman candle, never again to be reassembled in their original form. The carburettor is worse. Tiny jets, pistons, springs, all previously slotted into miniscule, irregularly shaped compartments, suddenly have no conceivable home or function, when exposed to the outside air.

Undeniably firm tapping with the back of a spanner is needed to get it all together again, just before the lawn-mower reconditioning craftsman appears. I leave him to it, for the sole reason that I do not wish to see the slowly gathering look of exultation on his face when he finds that an unqualified improver has bin fiddlin' abaht wiv the carb so now it's a write-off and a replycement'll tyke six . . .

He's got it going, on my return. But it will go only at full throttle, screaming on the very edge of disintegration. He shouts soundless instructions. I bawl inaudible thanks. He appears to have a moment of compassion, then remembers he has another job to do and goes.

Up and down the velvet sward, swerving, leaping, skidding, banking at either end in tight, 45-degree turns that leave long, bleeding furrows in the grass. Hands over their ears in fear for their brains, people appear at windows, making panic-stricken, silent mouthings for peace. Like Nijinsky, whipped on, up, down, around by his private demon, I leap, skid, slip, speed on behind the incandescent howling machine. . . .

Someone once said, complaining of a collection of my pieces, 'How he loves disaster.'

Disaster, whacker, is a naturally intrusive element. It's standing slightly to one side, watching it while it blows its head off, that creates a kind of affection for the crazy old jade.

41

Trial Run in Revolution

THE external glow of the caravanserai promises, despite its proximity to the Slough Trading Estate, high carnival within.

A white, Spanish-type structure, wrought-iron accessories, Riviera red-tiled roof, neon signs announcing Swimming Pool, Ballroom, Restaurant, American Bar, and all round it, jammed hub to hub, a mass of wealthy, glittering, two-tone automobiles.

All this leaps out of the night, with the impact of a Hollywood production number. Whatever is going on inside, it's fiesta. Floor-show by Sinatra. Beautiful, Brazilian-style persons of all sexes dancing a staccato-Cha-cha-cha in semi-darkness. Interior décor of giant rubber plants and other tropical, housebroken foliage. Waiters in white mess-jackets sliding about with silver trays of Daiquiris and mint juleps. The clack of maraccas and a Latin-American combo in frilly red shirts giving out with subdued Olés. . . .

Perhaps something more Nordic, owing to the proximity of the Slough Trading Estate, but with all those cars outside whatever is going on inside must at least present some cocktail of life, colour, variety, laughter, some adrenalin injection invigorating at ten o'clock at night to a dinnerless man whose mind has been reduced to the size and texture of a split-pea by the rigours of writing for children's television.

Brisk as a wildebeeste making for the water-hole, I speed into the American Bar—and find that it's absolutely empty. There's no one there at all, save for a ginger-haired lad in a hospital orderly's white coat, fiddling despondently with a couple of cocktail sticks behind the counter.

The shock is profound. It's like driving into a city at night, shop windows, street lights ablaze, cars lining the pavements, but all trace of human life has fled, from some unimaginable terror. Something like that must have happened here. A mass sabotage of the cars outside so that the owners have abandoned them, and walked home? An armed hold-up, so that all the guests are locked in the cellar and this ginger-haired lad, an accomplice, has been left on guard . . . ?

All at once, I become aware of an extraordinary vibration, a physical sensation, in the air. It's a roar of sound, a roar so all-pervading, like the thunder of Niagara, as to be inaudible until specifically listened for. It's coming through an open service hatch in the wall. It's coming from hundreds of men, in dark business suits, eating in the next room. They're packed so tightly shoulder to shoulder at long, trestle-like tables that the first swift impression is one of the dining-hall in Wormwood Scrubs. But these are genial, happy men, all bawling together at the same time.

Involuntary astonishment is rewarded by the ginger-haired barman. He reveals that it's a cricket dinner, and that the gents are celebrating the opening of the season. Even at this moment the President or the Captain or the Chairman or somebody is rising to his feet to say a few words.

All those glittering motor-cars. Life, colour, variety. The clack of maraccas, the staccato Cha-cha-cha? Ha-ha-ha. . . .

Persons dinnerless at ten o'clock at night after the rigours of writing for children's television can tend towards a fretfulness, a petulance otherwise foreign to their natures, particularly when they feel themselves to have been deceived, cheated, sucked in. 'That's jolly good news,' I tell the barman, 'when the whole external appearance of the joint led me to suppose that Sinatra was singing here tonight, to an audience of beautiful, Brazilian-type . . .'

Through the hatch comes the sound of hissing steam, or of a soda-water siphon, but it's neither of these things. It's a cricketer, glaring in outrage, and shushing me into silence! Shushing *me* into silence when I'm merely having a quiet drink by myself in the American Bar, which is open to and free for the use of all persons in funds and of sober demeanour. Shushing *me*, when it's all I can do to formulate whatever thoughts I wish to convey to the barman for the yelping pandemonium of laughter with which their blinking dinner is greeting the mildest witticism on the part of the President or the Captain, or whoever he may be. Do they suppose they have bought the entire establishment? Do they mean that while their President or their Captain or their third reserve wicketkeeper is cracking jokes comprehensible only to their own enclosed circle that persons as far as Bletchley must fall silent and . . .

The glaring cricketer shushes me again. Inadvertently, I must have allowed a stray phrase of these speculations to become audible. Other outraged faces are turned towards the hatch. Cowardice, rather more than any live-and-let-live policy, decides me upon silence and withdrawal to a corner of the bar well away from the possibility of direct fire, going in or coming out.

Revolutionaries, underdog supporters, principle defenders, Establishment upsetters must have the courage of lions, to fight their good fight. Perhaps this is why passive resistance is catching on so rapidly. It gives you a chance to see if you like the battle, before the danger arises of getting hurt.

42

All in an Ant-proof Metal Box

WHY don't Charles Clore, Jack Cotton, Isaac Woolfson, Bernard Sunley, Simon Marks—fill in your own favourites—stop?

Why, if you could cash in today the stocks, shares, premises, machinery, prospects and goodwill, the care of which keeps you wide awake throughout the livelong night in a timbered manse in Sunningdale, don't you do it?

What is this Knoxian, Calvinist hair-shirtery that stops a man who finds he's got a million saying: 'And about time too. I propose now never to do another stroke of work again.'

Regard the case of Douglas Collins. He makes a fortune from cosmetics, finds that's too easy, takes on the film business, survives, find he's got a million and retires. But not into idleness. He resolves to write at least 1,000 words of his autobiography every day, before turning to whatever relaxations his savings can provide. This masochism is actually commended by a daily newspaper, which takes the trouble to point out that while it is pleasant to stand on the pinnacle of success, even more rewarding is the day-to-day struggle to achieve it.

Balance this against a statement made to me the other evening by a citizen of middle years wearing a cream silk shirt and hand-made shoes. 'Do?' he replied to my penetrating enquiry. 'I'm glad to tell you I'm so rich I don't do anything. I have many interests, however, like art, literature and the theatre. I'm more or less expert at tennis and golf. I'm flying to Rome tomorrow for a party which promises to be rather fun, and then I'm going on to Cannes because they're putting two new engines into my yacht. I'm in the best of health,' he added, in case I was worried, 'and my only complaint is that the days—and the nights—are too short for my needs.'

Good, clear thinking, marching on absolutely parallel lines with my own. Give me £100,000 in single notes in a strong, ant-proof and fire-proof metal box, a modest little shopping yachtie off the Côte d'Azur, and I shall trouble the world no longer.

But look at the clatter of objections that such a simple proposal provokes.

'The frightful people you'd have to live with. All those dull millionaires, the spongers, the layabouts. They'd only be sucking up to you for your money——'

They'd go pretty dry. Here's Mr. Sponger and his doxie, Miss Layabout, coming aboard.

'Good morning,' says the free man with the ant-proof box. 'Don't bother to sit down,' he says, adding a fragrance of cognac to his breakfast coffee. 'There is no gravy for you today, unless you can amuse me—or illuminate my mind. Try. I've got the whole glorious sunlit day before me, and nothing else to do. Although it's possible,' he adds fairly, 'that I may suddenly cast off and go to Portofino or Ischia which will cut your efforts short, because you'll be going ashore.'

There would be no trouble—free airline tickets would bring them in a flash—about finding companions of the right sort—i.e. those imaginatively equipped to derive unclouded pleasure from sitting in hot sunshine, drinking wine and speculating with a proper admixture of irony upon the nature of human kind, with special reference to those who believe that work brings happiness, while running for a bus up Tottenham Court Road in sleet provoked by a north-east gale.

Lunch drifting by to five o'clock, and the only grit in the whole situation being the minimal labour involved in lowering the speedboat, to fly across the wine-dark sea to St. Tropez, where we might have a look at Bardot and her little playmates having *Welt*—or, more probably, personal—*Schmerz* in the glittering *boites* of the town.

'But,' cry the Knoxian, Calvinist hair-shirters, 'you'd be bored to tears in no time if you had no work to do——'

Regard the workless man, coming up on deck to a hot, brazen sky. Not a ripple on the water, scarcely a ripple on the soul. Breakfast waits under the awning. He'll be driving to Nice Airport round about midday in a white Alfa Romeo, to meet friends with minds like knives who are flying in from London for a fortnight's cruise to Capri, and if too many of the boys are there what in the world is the matter with Corsica? Crippling boredom, if weighed against the Underground clattering into Cannon Street, umbrellas, wet newspapers, the office, someone's lost the invoice, phone call from the bank manager because no one wants our galvanized-iron buckets and in any case all the workers in the factory will shortly be coming out on strike.

The Calvinists last strike. 'But if you had £100,000 in an ant-proof, fire-proof metal box you'd be worried to death that someone would steal it.'

I wouldn't mind worrying about that at all. The top of the box would be upholstered in velvet and I'd sit on it in the sunshine, slowly mulling over the advisability of turning all those lovely singletons into travellers' cheques. . . .

Just give it to me, and I'll do the rest. And in the meantime, Douglas Collins, stop tormenting yourself with writing.

You're making me feel tired.

43

A Pause in the Lemming Ride

THE Motor Commuters roar along Western Avenue, steel-clad, ruthless, weaving and jinking for position, an armoured, unstoppable horde charging down upon the defenceless city—except that the city is stuffed nearly to bursting already, so that the whole force of this flying assault will be quietly absorbed, like water into blotting-paper, by the clotted, shockproof jam at Shepherd's Bush.

Despite the certainty of this ultimate defeat all the Motor Commuters are determined to reach it before the others, jostling, hooting, belting their machinery, uttering profane prayers that the slob in front won't stop, trying to turn right, so that all the cunning ferrets on the inside slip past, skating through the next lot of traffic lights. . . .

They don't look at one another, the Motor Commuters hurtling along bumper to bumper, even when a new block stops them cheek by jowl and there's Genghis Khan beside you who slammed past on the Northolt straight with a blast of his horn which has certainly laid the foundations of coronary thrombosis in the years, if any, to come.

No flicker of recognition or of apology. Both Commuters, the doer and the done, sit there at the wheel, an arm thrown with the insouciance of Madame Recamier along the back of the passenger seat, looking straight ahead through the windscreen in quiet reverie, as though contemplating the unpredictable shadings of nature from a vantage point on Box Hill. Both radios are playing, 'Housewives' Choice' . . . *so come along with meee to my little corner of the world . . .*

The block clears. Shove, threaten, push, foot flat down and we're off again.

Sometimes an unfledged warrior, green to the game, is driven to give tongue. At the roundabout a solid financier in a pale-beige Rolls crowds a youth in a home-made Austin Seven—home-made, by the look of it, out of biscuit tins. The youth has a fearful ginger moustache, a red and white striped woollen cap with a bobble on the top, but no sense of inferiority. 'Don't scratch that, acker, until you've paid for it!' he bawls. The financier makes a brief, unpleasant gesture and sweeps away.

One of the difficulties I face—in addition to that of remaining alive—in this headlong lemming ride is the frequent need to buy an ounce of tobacco of a kind not readily available at the other end, and this involves a disagreeable change in personality.

The Motor Commuter, commuting, is a steely automaton, asking no quarter and giving none. Once he stops, however, he disintegrates, shorn of plumes, tusks and spurs. . . .

Having stopped, for a crumb of golden shred, I'm still parked beside the kerb. The Commuters roar past, three abreast, jaws clamped, eyes glittering, functional cogs tightly enmeshed, all helplessly for one and one for all. I put out an appealing hand, indicating my desire to leap back again into the maelstrom, and snatch it in as a Jag knifes by with howling horn.

Put the whole face out of the window. A servile, slippery smile, trying to make contact with one of the hurtling Commuter Automata—just a flick of human feeling that will cause him to lift his foot for a split-second, creating a sudden gap into which I can enmesh myself at peak revs, up like lightning through the cog-swaps and belt on.

Actually, the servile, slippery smile has proved so wearing that I've been compelled to patronize a tobacconist in a quiet side road, off the main stream, and a curious situation has broken out there.

The shop—it's also a newsagent's—is staffed by three middle-aged ladies. They wear pink, nylon overall coats with home-made cardigans shining through in shades of plum and navy blue. They have a kind of pasteurized, dehydrated Bohemianism about them, a skimmed-milk raffishness. Cigarettes always dangle from the corners of their mouths. One of them has gone mad and tried a henna rinse without adding water. They're like barmaids in an amateur dramatic society's conception of a pub. They call everyone dear. It must be the atmosphere of the shop that does it—all those cigarettes and hair-clips and whiffs and the women's magazines on the counter telling them how to get and hold their man. . . .

And I—I say it without immodesty—have become their prince, their dream-boat, their roving sailor boy whose fleeting, unpredictable visits throw them into a state of accelerated heartbeats, hot flushes, steamed glasses, though I'm more than ready to admit that the rest of their clientele seems to be exclusively female, with string bags and in patchy health, and given to chronic complaint and surgical anecdote.

They go at it in chorus. 'Fancy, look who's here again!' 'Same as usual, dear?' 'Don't tell me, I know . . .' I can do nothing in the face of such tender homage but play back to it. 'Too kind, ladies. And who's wearing the doe-eyed look? Vairy effective. And what about that hair? And silver nail-varnish! Whatever next . . . ?'

It's hard, slogging work, specially when you need a whole new set of more or less pharmaceutical *plaisanteries* at least three times a week. Not that I go in there very often now. After a dice with the Commuter Automata all the way from Denham one simply doesn't feel up to giving so much.

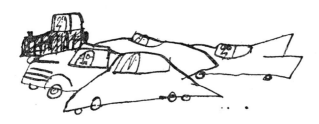

44

Ireland's Different to England, See?

THE summer was in progress one morning last year in the village of Rooskey, on the River Shannon in Co. Longford. The rain was descending vertically on the deck of a cabin-cruiser in which, at the early hour of 9.45, I was taking breakfast in bed.

All at once, unexpected as the roaring of a lion, an English accent established itself on the jetty. 'I say!' it cried. 'I say, is anyone there?'

We love strangers in Ireland. You never know what they're going to be like. With high expectation I drew back the six inches of chintz concealing the port-hole, and there he was—a splendid specimen of English holiday male, fully grown, with all his distinguishing marks ablaze.

He wore, in the downpour, his wife's transparent plastic mackintosh and a transparent pixie hood. Under the mackintosh I could see a striped, Shaftesbury-Avenue-Italian jersey and a pair of white shorts. On his feet he wore yellow socks and new, brown leather sandals. 'I say,' he called. 'I say, is anyone there?'

I let him know, through the port-hole, that a fellow human was present, while warning him that it was practically the middle of the night. 'Or perhaps,' I said, 'you're still on the way to bed.' There had been, the previous evening, a grand gala ball in aid of the Church in a fancy palais called Dreamland on the other side of the river which had terminated round about 4 a.m., a normal social occasion in Irish rural life.

He knelt down on the jetty, presenting me with a close-up through the frame of the port-hole of the pixie hood, and a pale, anxious face. 'Hello, there,' he said. 'Actually, I was looking for some milk.' He held up a small, plastic jug, making his mission clear. The rain poured into it, as though from a tap.

We love strangers in Ireland. It's the last place left in the British Isles where you'll find a deeply appreciative audience if you want to talk about yourself. I invited him to fill in the details of how he came to be standing on Tony Fallon's jetty at the stark hour of 9.45, wearing a pixie hood and carrying a plastic jug.

He provided some facts. He was cruising with his wife and family, and had made an early start, to cover twenty miles before breakfast, as they had only a week and wished to see as much of the Shannon as possible in this short space of time. His wife and children were very hungry, but they couldn't start breakfast until they had some milk. He gestured with the jug towards Tony Fallon's. 'The shop,' he said, 'doesn't seem to be open.'

It's always a pleasure to us in Ireland to give information to the stranger, because he can scarcely ever believe his ears.

'Owing to the licensing laws,' I said, 'the shop doesn't open until the legal hour of 10.30, but when it does you'll be able to buy not only a bottle of milk but also a packet of aspirin, a bar of cut-plug, a tin of peaches, a rat-trap, a screwdriver, half a pound of streaky bacon, a length of clothes-line, a jar of honey, a fishing rod, a morning paper and a bottle of stout with which to wash it down. What's more, Tony's got a piano in the back lounge so that while waiting you'll be able to play and sing. In addition, you'll be able to deal in all these commodities and pleasures for thirteen hours without a break, because the place doesn't shut until 11.30 tonight.'

'I see,' he said, though the concept was obviously new to him. 'I suppose,' he suggested after a moment, 'there isn't a sort of dairy where I could just buy a bottle of milk?'

'There's one on the other side of the river,' I told him, 'but you'd have to walk nearly half a mile in the rain, and then it mightn't be open. The butcher, for instance, only comes to

Rooskey once a week, and then he chops up carcasses in a rented sitting-room, with floral paper on the walls. Ireland's different to England, you see. The individual runs the country here, not the country the individual, and no individuals are up and about yet, so if I were you I'd go back to bed until they get the place aired.'

Ireland is beautiful to look at, the beauty of desolation. Long, white roads, the only traveller for miles an old woman in a black shawl on a donkey cart. The light is ever changing on the distant mountains, as the tall clouds sail in from the Atlantic. There is complete silence. A curlew pipes suddenly, but there is nothing else. A shaft of sunlight turns the bog to gold. Then the clouds darken again over the purple hills and the soft rain comes down and everything turns to pearly grey and luminous green. Machines and houses, brick walls and concrete and barbed wire died out before they got here. It's the uttermost, empty edge of Europe, the silent, prehistoric land of Hy Brazil. It makes a haunting, quite unforgettable impression even on jolly, orange-sucking coach-parties from Manchester, Scunthorpe and Hull, so that once bitten by it they always come back, to recapture the strange feeling of being one's own man in a lost and dream-like world, where there's no need to do anything in a hurry because you can be perfectly certain that no one else will be there to do it for or with you . . . until we've got the place aired, and then there's a fair chance there'll be no need to do it at all.

It's a slowing down of the tempo that the English find difficult to get in step with at first, and even when they find the beat they're never quite happy, being a people over-concerned with immediate practicalities, but on the other hand it provides them with an experience they never forget.

Take, for instance, the case of this milk-hunting Englishman. I went over to Tony Fallon's pub at about eleven o'clock, having a number of urgent commissions on my mind, to find him, still in his pixie hood and transparent mac, stamping up and down the light hardware and tinned comestibles department of the shop, and still calling, though on a more strained note than before, 'I say, there—I say!' He had his plastic jug with him, but it was empty.

He was glad to see me. 'I say,' he said, 'there seems to be no one here. A girl opened the shop at half past ten, but she's disappeared.'

I was able to clarify the position. 'Our genial host,' I said, 'Mr. Tony Fallon, is heir-apparent to the resident undertaker, so he's gone to a funeral to polish up his technique with the ropes that go round the coffin. The beautiful girl who opened the door is his sister Patty, and she is now putting ten gallons of petrol into a lorry across the road, because Tony Fallon owns the filling station as well. She may be there for some time because the lorry driver has just arrived from Belturbet and she has a natural desire to know what's going on in a metropolis of that size. I don't know where Mrs. Fallon is, but she's got two small children, and is probably attending to them. Have a bottle of stout.'

'But I haven't had breakfast yet,' he said. 'We've no milk.'

I went into the bar at the back and pulled two bottles of stout, leaving the money in an ashtray. 'But what about breakfast?' he said. 'We want to get provisioned up, and make a start——'

'If you're going downstream,' I said, 'there's no point in leaving now because I'm meeting the lock-keeper here at midday, and giving him a lift. He's seventy-eight, but he's never been in a cabin-cruiser and wants to broaden his mind. He might be here earlier, but that won't help because we've lost a child and can't start without her.'

He became over-concerned with practicalities. 'You've lost a child! Where? How? Have you told the police?'

'The police,' I said, 'are in the back bar. He's having a bottle of stout and reading the paper. The child went into Longford on the nine o'clock bus to buy some comics—she hates boats. She should have been back here by ten, but she didn't arrive, so she's obviously lost.'

He forgot about his milk troubles. 'What are you doing about it?'

'Nothing,' I said. 'She's got plaits and she's wearing leopard-skin trousers. Someone in Longford is bound to fall into conversation with such an interesting-looking visitor, and then they'll ring up about her. What I'm really worried about is getting some flexible cable to repair the steering gear, but the police thinks he knows a man in Mohill who might have some, so we're going there as soon as Tony comes back from the funeral with the car. There's one little difficulty about the car. Tony's just sold it, in his function as garagist, to a man who's coming to collect it, but if he turns up before we leave for Mohill he can take us there himself.'

He sifted through it, and came up with a matter which he considered affected himself. 'This lock-keeper,' he said. 'Do you mean I can't get through the lock without him? We wanted to start in about ten minutes.'

'You'd better have another bottle of stout,' I said. 'The lock-keeper is coming up from the lock in the Tourist Board's waterbus, because it can't get past here until the lock-keeper opens the swing bridge. He doesn't want to come up on his bicycle because he's going back to the lock with me. But in any case,' I said, 'there's no great hurry because a man's dropping in here on his way to Sligo to show me some new charts of the river, and there's a strong rumour that he broke down last night in Mullingar.'

'I see,' said the Englishman. 'I think,' he said tightly, 'I'd better go and tell my wife.'

It turned out to be a wonderful day, the kind of day you get only in Ireland, where past, present and future, and day and night, blend into an endless, whirling dream, into which new characters constantly intrude and stay awhile and vanish, un-explained—a dream of comings and goings and long talks with total strangers, of songs and loud laughter, of sudden friendships with people that know no class, where caste and snobbery are entirely unknown, and everything wrapped in this feeling of timelessness and buoyant, floating ease.

The Englishman, the lock-keeper, the policeman, the post-man and I spent a good deal of it in the distant town of Mohill, negotiating for flexible steel cable in perhaps twelve different pubs. When we got back to Rooskey the lock-keeper opened the swing-bridge for the waterbus. We stood on it, while he wound the handle, wondering at the power of machinery. In Tony Fallon's we found that the Englishman's wife and my wife had set off in a speedboat at thirty-five knots for Carrick-on-Shannon, piloted by the man who was on his way to Sligo. He had, it seemed, been compelled to make a detour, for business or social reasons, to Longford, where general rumour quickly led him to a child in leopard-skin trousers, contentedly browsing in a book-shop, having spent her return fare.

'That,' as I explained it to the Englishman, 'is the wonderful thing about Ireland, our passionate interest in life, and in human beings. For twenty miles all up and down the river people have heard there are two cabin-cruisers in Rooskey, and there's a young one missing, in leopard-skin trousers. A man we met in Mohill passed it on to a fella in Drumlish, who met another fella at the crossroads in Ballinalee, so it's a wonder they hadn't heard in Longford that a tiger was loose from the Dublin Zoo. I bet you,' I said, 'there's fellas as far away as Sligo town itself who have heard there might be a bit of a do tonight in Tony Fallon's, and they're coming here now by way of Galway.'

A car pulled up at the filling station. A head came out of the window. It was a man I hadn't seen for ten years. 'I heard,' he said, 'below in Athlone you were up this way. Are you buying?' We brought him inside.

Timelessness and buoyancy and ease. The wives and the man with the speedboat came back and he played the piano so they started another gala ball in the back room. A middle-aged and studious American couple came in, Pennsylvania Quakers by persuasion, touring Ireland in search of Celtic crosses. Within a few moments they were absorbed in conversation with a very old farmer whose brother, during the Jimmy Walker administration, had been a policeman in New York. There was a Swedish couple as well, who suddenly materialized from the wind and the rain of the Irish night. You'd have thought the whole world was gathered together. By 11.30, and closing time, the back room and the bar and the shop were packed so tightly we could only stand, shoulder to shoulder, and sing. And it had really all begun twelve hours ago with an Englishman, in a pixie hood, looking for a small jug of milk.

That's what happens in Ireland, where the machines and mass entertainment haven't reached, where every man is his own man, and makes the day go by as he wishes.

It's what people come to Ireland for. They're under pressure, now, everywhere else.

45

Mother—I'm Back!

WHAT we're liable to get for Christmas this year is a tiny tartan bag containing three pencils in the form of miniature golf-clubs, another one, and a net made of string to be hung between two chairs, on which woollies can be dried without losing their shape.

What we want for Christmas is a new parlour game, and I've got it—a divertissement so richly satisfying that I can't imagine how I came to invent it with such ease, round about two o'clock on the morning of Boxing Day last year.

We'd just passed through the unspeakable degradation of charades, the last one, presented by an aunt of mine and two helpless victims called Burke, being a true collector's piece in the field of dramatic paralysis.

My aunt, a slow-change artiste of infinite jest, whom Fate had tricked out of going on the boards professionally in 1902, came in with a look of profound solemnity, wearing a deerstalker with the flaps down and one of my shirts, overhanging a pair of dress trousers tucked into red and white hooped football stockings, an ensemble which could only have been based on the Eton Wall Game, though I was certain she'd never heard of it.

She was followed by Mrs. Burke, a rather smart but tense little woman with the bright, staring eyes of a bush-baby, now hopelessly unbalanced by a man's tweed cap, pulled low down to her eyebrows, with the peak standing out sideways over one ear. She might just conceivably have represented Jackie Coogan wearing a black net cocktail dress, a swoop into transvestism too beastly to invite analysis.

Behind her, after a long interval, came her husband, a deeply serious and thoughtful lecturer on economics. On his head he wore a pith helmet with a single paper rose protruding from one of the ventilation holes in the crown.

They arranged themselves in a line in front of us, my aunt struggling unsuccessfully to restrain her laughter at the inspired humour of her disguise, while the Burkes looked like the victims of a firing squad composed of maniacs, who'd compelled them to don fancy dress, in which to meet their end.

We gave them a scatter of applause.

My aunt took a pace forward. 'First syllable,' she announced with extreme solemnity, indicating that she had momentarily stepped out of character, and that we were not to assume that this was part of the show.

She rejoined her familiars. 'Now,' she said, in a hoarse whisper. Slowly, she raised her right hand in the V-sign. With the other she removed an imaginary cigar from the general area of her face, which she'd inflated into global form. The Burkes did likewise, Mrs. Burke, through nervousness, using the V-sign to remove her cigar, an effective economy which, I was surprised to find, had not occurred to me as a *modus operandi* before.

My mother, having given the demonstration insufficient thought, called out, 'Churchill!' Mr. Burke seized swiftly and thankfully on this release. 'That's it,' he said, and immediately removed his pith helmet.

But it wasn't, as we learnt from my aunt, without further delay. It wasn't Churchill at all, despite the powerful supporting evidence. It turned out, in a long and peevish altercation between the players, that what they were really doing was 'hat', the first step on a colourful programme leading to a grand finale in a modiste's, where clues were to have been laid that would have led us to 'hat-box', if our wits had been razor keen.

'We were only doing Churchill,' my aunt cried, 'to throw you off the scent!' The fury of her indignation was in no way impaired by the insanity of her dress. 'Churchill wears funny *hats*, doesn't he?'

No one seemed to find this explanation fully satisfying, specially my mother, a long-time admirer of Sir Winston's. 'What's the idea, then,' she asked truculently, 'of the football socks? And Sir Winston never had his shirt hanging out in his life.'

Victor Burke ventured a thought. 'Possibly,' he said, 'a black coat and striped trousers would have been more in character.' The memory of that rose-tipped pith-helmet was going to come between him and the laws of supply and demand for a long time to come. Mrs. Burke was encouraged by the firmness of his stand. 'Honestly,' she said, 'I'm quite sure Sir Winston doesn't wear caps and if he did they'd be straight.' Her Coogan image must suddenly have given her another stab. 'It's impossible,' she snapped, 'to act properly if you're wearing the wrong clothes. . . .'

It was at that moment I invented the new parlour game. It sprang into my mind, round and complete, the perfect antidote to the squalid incompetence of charades. 'That's it!' I cried. 'You've got it, duchess! There's no proper acting in charades. We're just clowning around, numb with incompetence and embarrassment, trying feverishly to be funny—an endeavour which has brought trained, professional comedians, skilled in every artifice of timing and technique, with a routine worked out to the last detail and someone to write their jokes. . . .' At this moment a bottle of cherry brandy which I happened to be holding started to play 'The Bluebells of Scotland'. I put it down quickly, stopping its nonsense before some fool started laughing. 'An endeavour which has brought trained comedians to bankruptcy, alcoholism and an early grave. If we want to act—and who doesn't at two o'clock in the morning—let us turn our talents to the exposition of tragedy, an infinitely easier ride.'

After a pause of a couple of seconds a young man called Tom something or other—living, I calculated, on borrowed time at someone else's family Christmas—suggested a game of Murder. 'Is that sad enough for you?' he said.

I put a stop to that. 'If you can stand being cross-questioned by a detective who keeps telling you he can't think of any more questions to ask, I can't,' I said. 'We'll try this. Each of us is going to go out of the room in turn, have a short period of meditation outside and then come in again, and with every crumb of heart, soul, spirit and imagination we can summon to our aid deliver just one line, and mean it. Let's see if we can really act, and not just muck about with pith helmets.'

They couldn't see it, though my aunt was eager to have a crack at anything that was going. 'How do you mean?' she said. 'What do we say?'

It burst, unbidden and unconsidered, upon my mind.

'Mother—I'm back!'

Although I say it myself it was, even without rehearsal, a beautiful rendition. There was deep pathos in it. There was love and homesickness and humility and contrition, and a melting sadness for the futility of all the wasted years. It got even the man who wanted to play Murder. 'Where have you been?' he asked respectfully.

'Imagine that for yourselves,' I told them. 'Twenty-five years in the Siberian salt-mines, or for the ladies a similar spell as the plaything, in mid-Sahara, of a licentious Arab sheik. The important thing is that you're back. You steal into the old familiar room and there is Mother, older and frailer now, but still bowed over her favourite spinning-wheel, just as she used to be. She doesn't see you. Her back is to the door. You approach her, and from the depth of your being you say, "Mother—I'm back!"'

Suddenly, they all wanted to do it at the same time, and I had to steady them down. It had occurred to me that we wanted a real mother, a bowed figure at the writing-desk, failing a spinning-wheel, who would turn in tremulous wonder as the long-lost child appeared, and give us something solid to play against. Unfortunately, as soon as my aunt saw that a slow turn and tremulous wonder were on the agenda she insisted on playing the mother herself, and disappeared for twenty minutes, to return with a black shawl over her head and burnt-cork lines on the face, a piece of up-staging so powerful that I decided to have first stab at the prodigal, to get the thing off the ground.

Outside the door I made the interesting psychological discovery that I was incapable of projecting myself with complete sincerity into the role of a middle-aged son returning to the old manse after—the scenario was sketchy even in my own mind—twenty years beachcombing in Tahiti. I felt merely like myself, about to try to justify a passing flight of fancy before some not entirely sober friends and relations who, judging by the roar of conversation coming from within, had already forgotten completely the modest entertainment promised by him without.

But that, I reasoned, was the actor's craft, to induce attention for a fiction in persons nine-tenths occupied with their own reality. Assuming an expression of melancholy—brow furrowed, mouth turned deeply down—I opened the door . . . and immediately went into a comic routine that would have disgraced a stand-in Widow Twankey at a Wednesday pantomime matinée in Pontypridd.

I got my finger stuck in the keyhole. I allowed myself to be assaulted, indelicately, by the door-handle. When the time came for me to deliver my line I seemed to be chewing gum. 'Mother,' I said, in a slow, Texas drawl, 'Ah'm Buck.'

It was nearly the end of the new game. Most of them believed it was a hoax, aimed at providing me with a solo comedy spot. I'd the greatest difficulty in persuading them to let me do it again. 'You've no idea,' I said, 'how difficult it is to project yourself with sincerity. And there's audience pressure, as well, and door-handling, composition of the features, the remembrance of things past. . . . It's fascinating. Watch this.'

Next time I got my melancholy going much better and quite unexpectedly added a piece of business that everyone later said was extraordinarily interesting—a defensive raising of the right hand, on the delivery of the line—'suggesting,' as someone said, 'you suspected that Mother's welcome home would be accompanied by the throwing of decayed fruit.'

After that they all wanted to do it, and they did it three or four times, each time revealing a new and more fascinating neurosis.

Little Mrs. Burke, on her first couple of runs, which were severely diluted by nervousness, merely chirped, 'Mother—I'm back,' as though she'd been round the corner for half a pound of streaky bacon. At the third attempt, however, she suddenly spat out, 'Mother—I'm back!' with such vicious resentment that Mother at the writing-table reared back in genuine fear.

The solid Victor Burke, on the other hand, produced his line practically in baby talk, suggesting that his image of the reunion was Mummy's enfolding arms, fortified with hot milk and rusks in front of the nursery fire, while the youth Tom, an operator of apparently draught-proof self-assurance, not only fell on his knees upon entering the room but also failed to get further than the word, 'Mother . . .' before being seized by a racking sob which, we were all agreed, owed nothing to artifice.

We carried on until five o'clock or so in the morning, all adding or subtracting minute nuances from our performances until they represented the final and definitive statement of the ego, and then we did it twice more each, to set the mould.

I can recommend 'Mother—I'm back!' for Christmas this year, in place of charades, but with one word of warning. Be careful to select for the part of Mother a friend or relative who, through diffidence or lack of ambition in the dramatic art, is content to confine her performance to a slow turn and tremulous wonder, or difficulties will ensue.

I myself was just coming in on Take Nine, ready for the charged pause after closing the door noiselessly behind me, when my aunt, who'd been getting fidgety over her admittedly modest responsibilities, suddenly swung round from the writing-table, flung her arms wide and cried in a voice sonorous with emotion, 'Rupert, my boy—you've returned!'

It would have taken Sir Larry himself, on a good night, to carry on from there.

46

Virtue Down the Pipe

A CLIMACTIC moment in the history of the Drama occurred on commercial television several weeks ago and as, after this long interval, it would seem that none of the paid critics noticed it, I advance with confidence into noticing it myself.

This was the plot—observed, admittedly, through a screen of cauliflower cheese and a rather bulky burgundy, in the lap—but it is, in essentials, correct.

Fred—I can't remember his exact name—works for an estate agent, but he's fiddling—a complex matter to do with knocking a couple of hundred off the purchase price and splitting the difference with the customer without telling the boss.

While engaged in this beastliness, Fred is also playing fast and loose with two girls in the office, as an appetizer to going home and rattling a tattoo on the shattered nerve ends of his poor wife, a creature demented by shortage of housekeeping money and a child who remains, in the interests, perhaps, of production costs and wear and tear on the director's nerves, permanently out of sight.

This is Fred's basic. In the course of the next forty minutes his behaviour gets even worse. He betrays his wife and the two typists by taking up again with a former *chere amie,* who is househunting. He fiddles the price of the house with her, to cover further obvious overheads, and the first of these misdemeanours is found out. Fred blames it on a junior clerk, who gets the sack.

Everything continues to go splendidly for Fred, to the peak point of a decision on the part of Mrs. Fred to go home to Mother for a week's rest, taking the invisible starveling with her, just at the moment when the reinstated crackling invites Fred to move into her apartment for the same period, but for a rather jollier break in routine.

I begin to get faintly worried. By my watch there are only five minutes left before the detergents foam in—surely insufficient time for Scotland Yard or other retribution to put the finger on Fred? But Mrs Fred starts a move in the right direction. . . .

She decides to cancel her visit to Mother, on the grounds that Fred looks worried—he could hit her—and that he needs her by his side—he could knock her cold. But Fred is an old campaigner. He begins to chat her up with sweet words. She must not think of him. She must take her little holiday, as planned.

Mrs. Fred, poor, guileless, drab, buys it. She touches his hand. 'You're so good to me, Fred. . .' she murmurs.

THE END

I couldn't believe it. I shot right up out of my chair, stunned with nutriment, but most of all by seeing the most sacred principle of the Drama outraged before my very eyes. Fred, rotten to the core, had got away with it! Evil had triumphed, leaving the sanctity of marriage, straight dealing on the part of estate agents and a number of other virtues derided and humbled in the dust!

I was genuinely and deeply shocked. I mean, one allows that the Lord Chamberlain has undoubtedly eased his stays over the presentation of extra-curricular work in the boudoir, and certain other forms of association one would not have seen in Daddy's day, but the fact remains that however merry and bright the malpractices they are always punished, in the Drama, in the end.

But here was licence run rife, rivers rushing backwards, a total reversal of everything that we, the audience, had ever known.

Why—I thought, my mind seizing upon the Western as the most obvious manifestation of the power of Good—why, it would be like Cheyenne suddenly kicking down the door of the

Blazing Gulch saloon and there inside are Judd Brewster and his gang of hired killers, all of whom need their hats reblocked and cleaned.

Cheyenne knows that they are plotting to dispossess little old frail Miss Emily, who is so kind to Apache orphans whose parents have written themselves off with Judd's fire-water.

'Reach, Judd!' says Cheyenne. 'It's the end of the trail.'

Judd laughs, a horrible sound. 'Don't be like that, Chey,' he says. 'Would ten thousand dollahs, cash, hush yo' mouth?'

Cheyenne ponders it in his slow way. 'Waal,' he allows, ten minutes later, 'Ah figure Ah talks a mite too much anyways. It's a deal.' He stashes his guns, pulls up a chair to the table and they all get stoned on sour mash. Fade out to a barber-shop chorus of 'Sweet Adeline'. Cheyenne and Judd have exchanged sombreros, while Miss Emily and her brood of orphans sob bitterly outside the window, lashed by heavy rain.

It's the greatest revolution in the Drama since Sam Beckett deprived it of plot. And look what it's going to do for plotting. None of that weary contrivance of retribution for the hero jewel thief.

This way, he finishes up as the heavily disguised proprietor of a decaying antique shop in Woodstock, married to the vegetarian daughter of a North Oxford don.

Morally, it may be unsound, but it's a lot truer to life.

47

A Quiet Time with Cantuar

'WHAT a tremendous achievement.'
'You've certainly got to hand it to the Russians.'
'What sublime courage.'
'A giant step forward in the progress of mankind.'
The clamour grows, all eyes turned upwards with newly aggressive intent to the suddenly habitable sky.

But stay! Who—what—is this, this apparently human figure, this decadent anchorite withdrawn from the general tumult, this bloodless *solitaire* who lies in the shade of the almond blossom, a lily hand around a glass of wine, solemnly speculating upon the configuration, state of repair and varied uses of his own bare feet?

While all this bawling about outer space is going on, *le solitaire, c'est moi.* The French results from a quick scuffle through the dictionary and the desire to express a sensation of reactionary remoteness, an eighteenth-century fastidiousness, a coolly intellectual withdrawal from, to, by or whatever it is, all hysterical brou-ha-ha about cosmonauts, rocketry, blasting off, zoning in, girdling the earth and launching an exploratory man-probe at that first space-repair depot to Venus which used to be known as the Moon.

No cheers come from beneath the almond tree for Major Yuri Gagarin or Academician Nesmeyanov or any other successful space scientist because while I can appreciate, in the abstract, the fact that they've done something which no man has done before, I remain briskly indifferent to the fact that they've done it.

It's as though I were sitting in the circus and Manuel and

Manuela, those death-defying aerialists, launch out upon the high wire eighty feet above our heads. Manuel, wearing a tiny roller-skate strapped to his nose, swoops down the wire, balanced upon his proboscis, while Manuela stands on his upraised feet, playing 'Come back to Sorrento' on an electronic piano-accordion.

'Well,' is my briskly indifferent comment, 'they'd certainly be a couple of stiffs if they hadn't learnt how to do it. Could we now have the stimulating and unpredictable activities of the clowns?'

This is not to say that beneath the almond tree all is passive, reactionary, old-fashioned, turned away from the realities of the world today. Time is being given, between more profound meditations, to the active formulation of propaganda campaigns, all of them aimed at those persons who have become wild with excitement at the imminent conquest of space.

The purpose of the propaganda will be to urge them to overcome any last-minute fears that they might develop, and take off for it at the very earliest opportunity.

Into the first moon-bus, for instance, I would usher all those who have ever been heard to say, 'It's jolly well not fair and if only I was given a fair chance I'd jolly well show you, them, him, her that I could jolly well . . .' Blast off, poor tormented friends, and make a new start on Mars, where the hostile complexities of life will be neutralized by the difficulties of keeping alive at all.

Into the next space-coach or, preferably, into one leaving at the same time, I would assist everyone who maintains that their naturally neurotic, ego-maniacal, petulant and dissatisfied attitude towards their existence is not their fault but is a fearful burden laid upon them by living in the Shadow of the Bomb. They'll have a chance to flower in the craters of the Moon, where the absence of gravity will ensure that nothing can be dropped on them whatsoever.

All these persons are natural space-cheerers, because they're unable to cope with what they've got. Fasten your seat-belts, cosmonauts, and happy landings, up the lugs in volcanic ash. If the power of suggestion still remains to me, taking my ease under the earthly almond tree, you will shortly be joined by all persons of ruthless ambition but limited competence who reach the heights by standing on the hands of those who derive pleasure and satisfaction from doing the actual work. They'll be right up there with you, if I have my way, with a double charge of liquid oxygen up their jumpers, or whatever the technical term may be.

Anxieties about loneliness or idiosyncrasy are suddenly assuaged by the discovery that no less a thinker than the Archbishop of Canterbury feels the same way, or at least approximately the same way. 'No human problems,' he announced, on his return from Uganda, 'are solved by going to the moon. People who are impressed by space have nothing else to think of, poor fellows.'

Greetings, Cantuar. We're nearly of the same mind.

When you retire it would be a privilege for me to move over, to make room beneath the almond tree, so that we can go into the matter in greater detail.

48

The Conference Man

And when they play
'Here Comes the Bride',
I stand outside,
Just a girl that men forget.

A LOVELY old melody. So it was for me for the best twenty years of my life, and basically I was glad to be passed over despite a certain morbid curiosity about what the consummation would be like.

To wrench the matter—and not, it would seem, a moment too soon—out of metaphor into fact, I worked for twenty years on terms of open affability with the editors of a number of newspapers and magazines without being invited by a single one of them to step into the sanctum sanctorum and join the editorial conference. Even the smallest pawns in the game got in from time to time, like the medical correspondent, the astrologer and the crossword-puzzle setter, but not me. Just a girl that men forget. . . .

One might wonder why, but I didn't. In the interests of self-preservation I worked hard to keep myself out of conclave.

In these best twenty years I was privileged to work under, or slightly to one side of, no less than eleven editors, a modest bag, perhaps, by Fleet Street standards, but more than enough for me.

It was always a matter of delicate, precision engineering to create the right emotional climate between master and man in which the master, though probably holding a low personal regard for the man's contribution, could be put under the curb of suspecting that his judgement might be at fault, so that both could go our separate ways without uncomfortable friction against the other. It was tiring work if you had to do it more than once a year.

When each new editor appeared he'd have the usual four to five days riffling through the pack of resident workers, discarding some of the more highly paid kings, queens and knaves and then drawing more of the same kind, from the newspaper he'd just left, or been bounced from, in order to refill his hand. My turn used to come early in the second week, and these encounters always took the same form.

The new editor began by shaking hands, and then saying that he didn't want me to feel uneasy about anything, a frank declaration that he knew that craven fear had been agitating my mind since the news of his appointment had come through. Next, he said he'd always enjoyed reading my stuff, and identified in some detail a piece I'd written for another publication about two years before without, however, venturing upon any mention of the regular contributions I'd been making to our own sheet in the meantime. I respected this as a courteous indication of his view that the newspaper which was responsible for two-thirds of my income was getting the waste product of what appeared to be a thriving industry. With the air now translucently clear he would invite me to propose, say, one idea for a working format which would give a new and wider scope to my inimitable style.

It was a moment too cut and dried for comfort, and I always tried to fray it about. I never, I went to considerable length to explain, seemed to get any ideas at all, or not ideas as such, like riding a penny-farthing down the Strand to prove that traffic moved more quickly a hundred years ago, or becoming an elephant boy for a week with Billy Smart, to find out if animals enjoyed circus training. Then, in case he snapped at either of these trifles, I hurried on into a dissertation about humour, showing that it was in an entirely separate category from all other newspaper work, a thing of mood and emotion and personal metabolism so fragile that it could be suffocated

altogether by, say, working too closely with the reporting staff
or, indeed, any other department. The difficulty was, I said, that I
myself never really realized I'd got hold of a humorous idea until
after I'd written it, a complication that made it impossible for me
to present the idea, as it were, in advance, though naturally there
were some subjects which were . . .

They were busy men, all those editors, and they were usually
prepared to cut it short, round about here. We would part
with expressions of our absolute confidence in the future, and
the promise that, while I would continue to contribute in the
same genre as before, both of us would make a special point of
concentrating on new ideas, and lob them backwards and forwards, by telephone, one to another. The important thing was
that it put paid to any thought of my joining the editorial conference. 'For what,' as I put it to one envious features man,
'conductor of an orchestra would tolerate a flautist sitting in the
front row who's come without his flute? And what flautist would
volunteer for fluting who doesn't know the score?'

All that was settled by my twelfth, and probably last, editor.
Starting with a quick rinse and reconstruction of the reporters and
the art department, he then issued a letter to all the features men
addressing us as his 'gifted writers', and begging us, if we could
spare the time, to attend upon him the following Wednesday
for the pooling and mutual fertilization of ideas.

It was a swift and deadly move, all the more effective for
having been made without warning. It caught me a severe clip.
I'd had no opportunity for climate construction, or the fraying of
clear-cut issues. It looked as though I'd have to produce ideas
instead. I found it small consolation to know that my curiosity
about what went on at editorial conferences would now be
settled. It might, I feared, be settled for good.

When Wednesday came, and the gifted writers started to
gather in the secretary's room, it was some comfort to find that
I was not the only one who'd been caught between wind and
water. A genial professional countryman, who up till now had

been happy to send in his jottings about grouse, badgers and the habits of the peewit by post, was profoundly alarmed at having to put in a personal appearance. 'What's all this about gifted writers?' he wanted to know. 'I'm a working journalist and I'd like to leave it at that.'

I shared his anxiety. 'If you're a gifted writer,' I said, 'you've got to write in a gifted way, and I'm not sure either of us is up to it. Have you got any ideas?' If, I thought, there was going to be pooling and mutual fertilization it might not be a bad idea to get off to a premature start, though my own game-bag was none too full.

He clammed up immediately. 'Not a sausage,' he said, clearly demonstrating the gifted writer's natural tendency to share his ideas with another.

We went into the editor's room. With every nerve alert to make an early assessment of the speed of the court, I saw that the question of seating was probably vital. There weren't enough chairs, so that at least three of the gifteds would have to sit on a side table, getting cramp, or lean against the wall, sliding off into vertigo. Furthermore, the sun was blazing in through the windows behind the editor's desk. Several gifteds, who'd made a wrong move, were already in bad trouble here, either gazing into the glare with brisk but stone-blind efficiency, or shading their eyes with hands or notebooks, under so much pressure already that I gave little for their chances. Riding off the fashion editress, I snitched a chair in the corner, with my back to the window, in the approximate position of left-half to the editor's centre-forward. It had several advantages, in addition to good visibility. It was a modest post, withdrawn from the central group, indicating more the observer than the active participator. It could also suggest, to those quick enough to spot it, that whatever other loyalties or alignments of interest might establish themselves the editor and I were, beyond question, playing on the same team.

The proceedings opened with the news editor reading out

from a typewritten schedule a list of stories upon which the reporters were already working. As we'd all been given a copy of this when we came in, and could read it for ourselves, its purpose might have been to show that hard news-gathering was already going on, and that it was up to the features men to match it, if we hoped to claim a space in the paper. We let it pass without comment.

The editor lit another cigarette and sat back with the relaxed air of a man who knows he's going to be amused and entertained to the point of surfeit. 'Well, chaps,' he said, 'let's hear all your ideas.'

I thought that silence would probably follow this, too, and was deeply shocked to see that nearly all the chaps, including the professional countryman, showed a positive eagerness to shove in their oar, apologizing briskly to one another for interrupting and then driving straight on, consulting copious notes and making it seem that the day would not be long enough in which to put forward all their ideas.

Nearly everyone had a new angle on the themes which were then current—the export of Irish horses and the breathalyzer for drunken drivers—and made their suggestions with such fire that the meeting became seriously animated—seriously, that is, for the man who had as yet made no contribution to it. I decided to rectify this with a light witticism from, as it were, the jester's privileged chair. 'How about,' I said, in a momentary lull, 'combining everything into one big story, and trying the breathalyzer on the Irish horses? I'm sure some of them could do with it. . . .'

Silence did follow this time. The silence of the tomb, and that's what it felt like. Buried, six feet deep. I had made a cardinal error, one of which only a man new to conference work could have been guilty—the error of getting yourself suspected, however unfairly, of regarding the conference as a load of bull's wool. My carefully chosen position, behind the editor and withdrawn from the other, honest workers, now seemed to add considerably to the general impression that I was merely sitting in for laughs. I tried to rectify it. 'I wasn't offering it,' I said, 'as a serious suggestion.'

The editor was politeness itself. 'What are you going to amuse us with this week?' he asked.

Under pressure, I made an even worse mistake, conference-wise, than the previous one. I started the speech-mechanism working without knowing what the end product was going to be. 'I met an interesting woman the other evening,' I said, 'who's built a swimming-pool in the basement of her house in the Boltons....'

The editor, and the conference, waited expectantly. As far as they were concerned the launching of this idea had got no further than a loosening of the first chock. 'I was just wondering,' I said, getting the whole vessel under way, 'what would happen if twenty thousand gallons started leaking out. It's a densely populated area. Douglas Fairbanks lives practically next door....'

The editor liked it. He liked it so much he took it away from me, and gave it to the news editor. 'Get one of the reporters on to it,' he said. 'There's a good news story there.'

I was so relieved to have made an acceptable contribution that I forgot, until the very end of the meeting, that I'd nothing to write about myself. The editor was unworried, eager to go into secret session with the advertising manager. 'You'll find something,' he said, 'all right.'

What I did find, three days later, was that the lady with the swimming-pool was so incensed by the suggestion that she was flooding the Fairbanks basement that she'd threatened to put the matter in the hands of her solicitors, if the slander continued. 'Do check your facts, cock,' said the reporter who'd run into it. 'It saves a lot of trouble in the end.'

To save trouble in the end—and because new ideas to give a wider scope to my inimitable style still obstinately refused to come—I remained almost entirely silent for the next three meetings, sitting modestly in the back row of gifteds, facing the full glare of the midday sun. At the end of the third one the editor said he'd reached the conclusion that inspiration probably came more easily to humorous writers when they were on their own, and that there'd be no need for me to attend on the following Wednesday.

The old half-back–centre-forward relationship had certainly broken up. A few days later it came to pieces altogether, with my being sent permanently off the field, but it didn't surprise me.

After twenty years on the touchline you're crazy to get into the game.